The Saints & The Poets

Shun Lee Fong

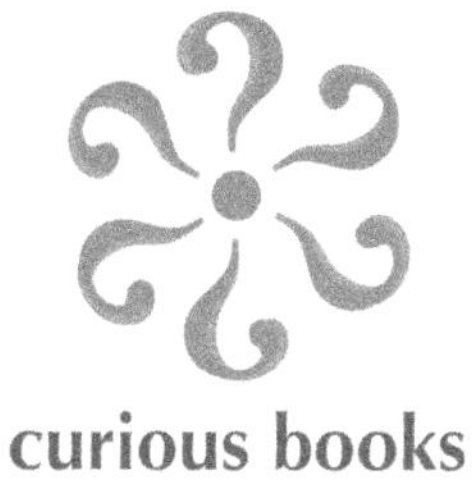

curious books

Curious Books
A division of Genuine Productions, LLC
5608 Saint Clair Avenue, Suite 105
Valley Village, California 91607

Printed in the United States of America

Curious Books Press Edition

ISBN-13: 978-0-9963675-2-3
ISBN-10: 0-9963675-2-7
Printing by The Card Shower, LLC - Anderson Print Group
6935 N. 97th Circle - Omaha, NE 68122

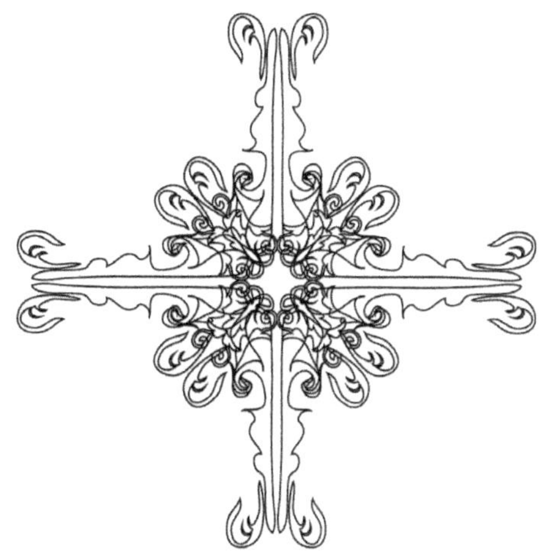

Table of Contents

Table of Contents, cont'd

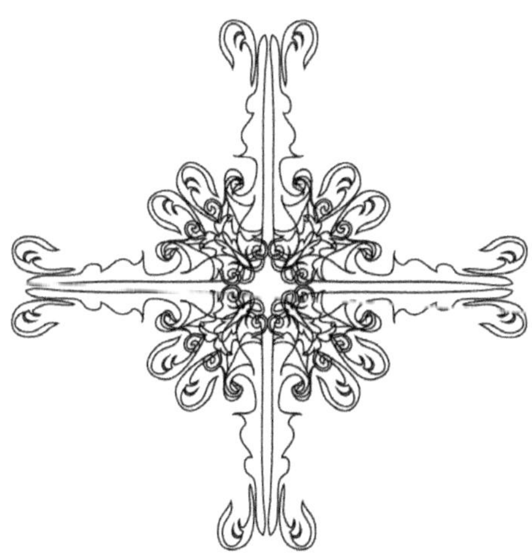

When the great history of trouble is written, my family will stand extremely high in the table of contents.

Allan Sherman
Comedy Writer, Television Producer, Singer & Actor

ACKNOWLEDGMENTS:

The fact that this book in now completed means I'm indebted to a tremendous number of people. Those who walked with me, those who cheered for me, those who prayed for me, those who gave wise counsel. To all the people who knew when to encourage and when to stay silent. Silence is often a wonderful gift for a writer who is mining the depths of his soul to say something worthwhile, and encouragement is the gift that keeps him digging. To all those who challenged my presuppositions and sharpened my thoughts and my words. There are always too many people for such a small space, but allow me to offer my thanks to a few:

To my parents for cultivating both the creative and the spiritual in me. When all is said and done, I hope that will be your legacy in me.

To all my siblings and their families for believing in the journey. Special thanks to my sister, Shun Sho, for all the work she put into the compilation, design, and illustrations she did for this book. Her perseverance is a large part of what made this book happen.

To Eric & Marnie Bents, Valerie Bourdain & Megan Bosselman, Caren Bream, Mike & Jenny Buckingham, Suzi & Miles Busby, Jeff & Diane Cahill, Brian & Ellen Chan, Jim & Karen Covell, John & Norma Donovan, Todd & Monica

Eby, Mike & Roberta Frank, Neal & Nancy Greenberg, Jim & Kathy Greve, Debbie Harmsen, Rob Helling, John & Barb Malek, Ray Mayhew, David McFadzean, Daryl & Sherri Newill, David & Joanne Norton, Jon & Linda Reid, Jeff & Sylvie Saxton, Susan Shepherd, Ken & Jonie Smith, Travis Vanderschaff, Chad & Candice Vice, Lori Walling-Fast, Paul & Jennifer Yoder, The Greenhouse leadership team, and many, many more.

Thank you to those who set me on the creative path: Bettelee Lewis, Thomas Crumb, Francis Wilson, David Klein, Fran Bates, Ann Bauer, Louise Roy, and many others.

An author is measured by the people who stand alongside him.

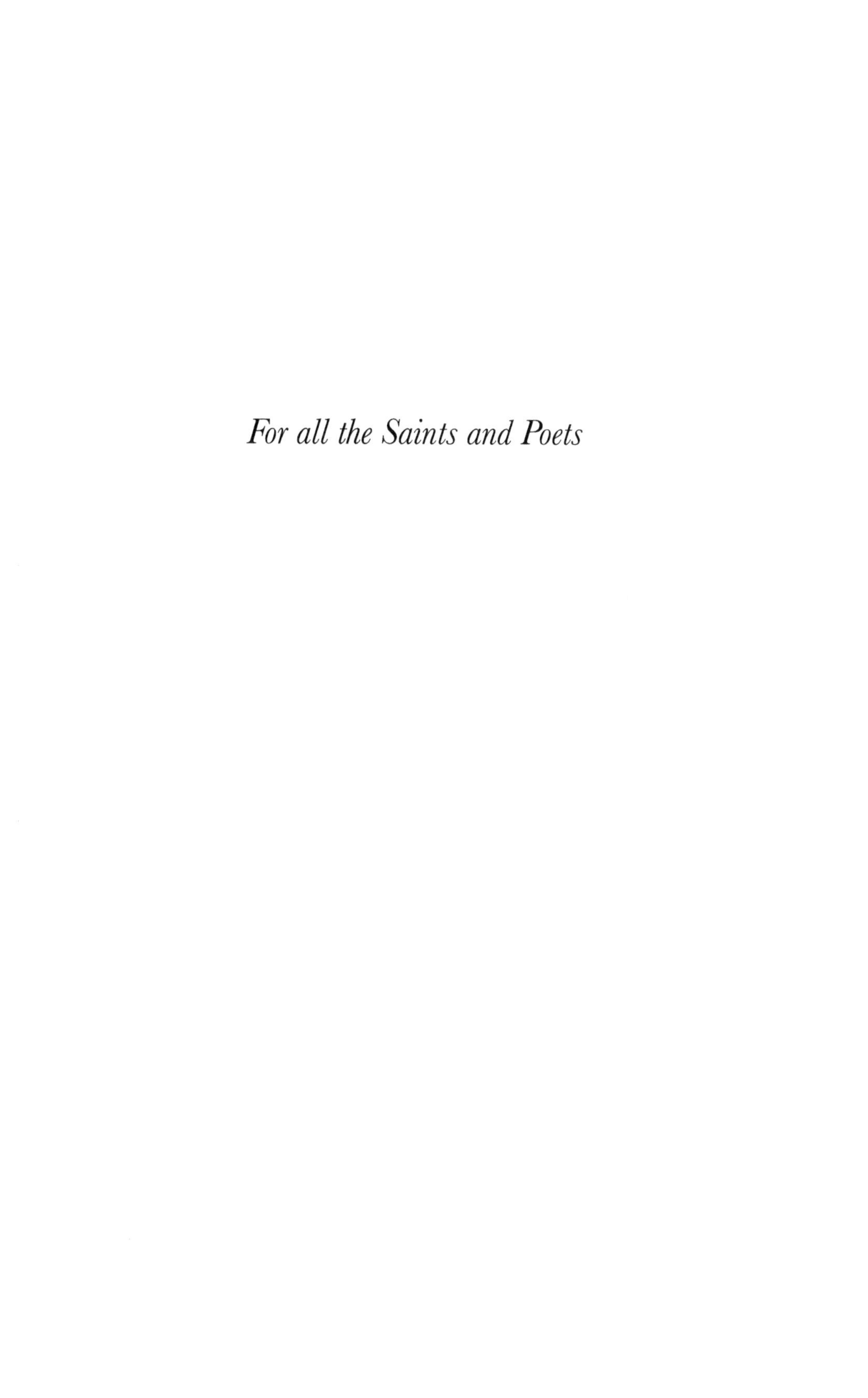

For all the Saints and Poets

EMILY:

Do any human beings ever realize life while they live it... every, every minute?

STAGE MANAGER:

No... the saints and the poets maybe, they do, some.

~ Thornton Wilder, *Our Town*

Foreword
The Invitation

Welcome to this conversation. Come on in, grab a cup of coffee, and get comfortable.

Oh, and make sure you have some paper and something to write with, because this won't be about me talking to you, but talking with you – a dialogue that hopefully will challenge both of us to do a little digging on our own.

After all, we're here because we are artists. Or maybe you're a creative person in general. Either way, you become more effective creatively as you do some healthy – and hopefully honest – self-examination. That's not to say that you should become overly interested in your self – but scrutinizing who you are and where you are in life will certainly propel you along this creative journey you find yourself on.

A little bit about me and this book may be in order so you know with whom you are dialoguing. For most of my life, I've been a creative artist – an actor, musician, writer, and film producer – and for nearly the last fifteen years, give or take, I've done so in a professional capacity in Hollywood, California.

I'm sure you may be asking yourself: Hollywood? Can anything good come from there? I hope you'll reserve judgment on that question until after you've made it through this book, keeping in mind that truth and beauty can come from the most unexpected places. After all, this rather skeptical question was asked about a little place called Nazareth too.

The writings you'll find here were not meant to be read all at once because they weren't written all at once either. Many of these were letters I wrote to various family and friends. Some were responses to letters that I've received from artists across the country. And I took a few of them straight from my own personal journal. I wrote all of them over the course of more than a decade as I have wrestled with one overarching question: What does it truly mean to be a creative person?

My hope is that you'll take the time to really wrestle with the same question, so I've laid this book out to be read over the course of a year. Of course, you can read it faster or slower as needed, or even jump around if you want.

I run my own media production company, Genuine Productions, LLC. I also help lead an incredible creative arts organization called The Greenhouse. The Greenhouse is an intentional community made up of all sorts of creative artists and entertainment professionals – writers and poets, actors and directors, photographers and painters, dancers and musicians, and many others – who cultivate an environment that's collaborative, effective, and full of life. It's a place where artists are encouraged to be artists, to be creative and to creatively serve one another and the culture around them. You can get plugged in too. Check it out at GreenhouseProductions.com.

Ultimately, art is a process. I've found that the responsibility of being an artist is a journey of the entire person. There is the learning, the understanding, and the doing – each of which requires its own kind of excellence. It's about more than just the product; it's also about the process that leads up to the product. It's my hope that this book will help you along that journey.

All my best,
Shun Lee Fong

1

My Motorcycle Diary

A couple years ago, I decided to take motorcycle lessons. Okay, I'll admit it: motorcycle lessons appealed primarily to my over-developed sense of adventure, but in my defense, it's not a bad skill for an actor to be able to list on his résumé. So I got all geared up and drove my car out to the nearby community college parking lot with visions of me whipping my bike around pylons with *Matrix*-like precision and ferocity.

Which is why it was a little disappointing that we spent most of the morning without even getting on the motorcycles. Eventually, however, the instructor let us start up the engines – only to direct us through a series of exercises in which we did nothing more than travel in a straight line. By that time, my *Matrix* pipe dream had vanished completely.

But then, suddenly, it was time to actually go somewhere. Since going anywhere is pretty much impossible without making some turns, the instructor also gave us this crucial piece of advice when it comes to steering, "Turn your head and *look*. You'll naturally steer in the direction your eyes follow. You'll go where you look."

Come to think of it, that's pretty good advice for just about anything in life, isn't it? We pretty naturally head towards what we keep our eyes on. What we pay the most attention to usually ends up being our destination. Maybe that's why King David, who was surrounded by all sorts of distractions as he wrote Psalm 141, said so decisively, "My eyes are fixed on you, O Sovereign Lord…"

We've got a brand new year here, an open road with the potential for some pretty amazing things for us as creative artists and as individuals. And with that potential comes a choice: You can choose to drive through this year in a basic straight line, essentially maintaining the status quo. Or you can give in to your own over-developed sense of adventure and actually go somewhere.

It's one of the most astounding opportunities you have, both in your relationship with God and in being an artist: *You can go as far and as deep as you want to.* But that choice is yours. And in a world full of all sorts of distractions, you will make your decision by the vision you maintain, by what you decide to keep your eyes on. You'll go where you look.

It's a brand new year stretching out ahead of us. And so, with my best Eastwood growl, let me take this opportunity to ask you: What are you looking at?

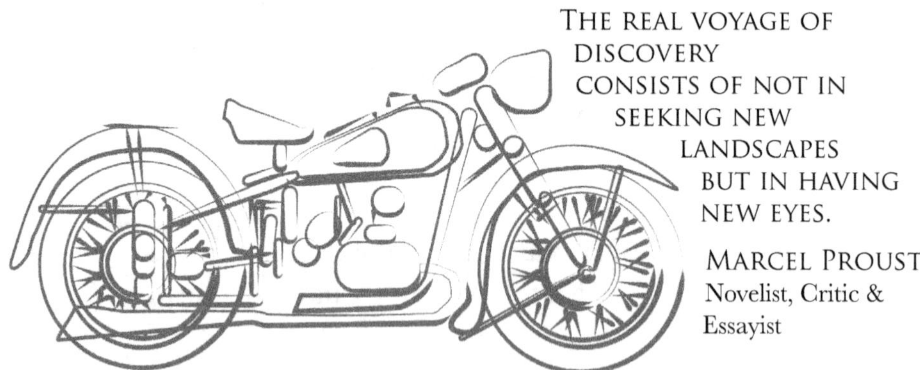

2

The Mission of the Saints & Poets

In one of my acting classes a while ago, my coach gave me a truth that sheds some light on our role as artists.

"We live," he said to the room full of expectant actors, "in a world that has forgotten how to feel. The world looks to you, as actors, to feel for them, to remind them what it is like to feel deeply. That is why they go to the movies and why they turn on the television every night. And that means that you, as actors, carry an awesome responsibility."

His assessment of our amnesia echoes the sentiments of artist Andy Warhol, who declared, "During the 1960s, I think, people forgot what emotions were supposed to be. And I don't think they've ever remembered."

Andy and my acting coach were right: we live in a world that largely has forgotten how to feel. And that leaves the world, and all of us who inhabit it, in a precarious position. If we have forgotten how to feel, we've lost the ability to engage with a God whose relationship with us is completed not only in our thoughts, but also in our emotions. How can a God who longs to comfort satisfy a world that has forgotten how to mourn? Of what use is a God of joy to a culture that is comfortably numb?

My acting coach was also right that artists – actors, painters, musicians, writers, poets, dancers, all the ones so prevalent and influential in our culture – bear a responsibility of helping the world to feel deeply again. But what will happen if they, too, forget how to feel? I think that Christians, and even more so, artists who are Christians, are charged with the weighty assignment of helping people become genuinely and deeply emotional again – without employing emotionalism – and to help them see the world once more, with feeling.

In the world of the comfortably numb, blessed are those who mourn, and blessed are those who can remind the world of true mourning… and true happiness, and true anger, and true jealousy, and true emotion of any sort.

Even more than that, though, is our charge to live our own lives deep in the currents of life's emotions as well – to "realize life" every minute, as Thornton Wilder once put it. This is the mission of the saints and the poets.

It is through this deep emotion that a heart that was once numb can so often directly receive the blessing of a living – and emotional – Father God.

THERE CAN BE NO KNOWLEDGE WITHOUT EMOTION. WE MAY BE AWARE OF A TRUTH, YET UNTIL WE HAVE FELT ITS FORCE, IT IS NOT OURS. TO THE COGNITION OF THE BRAIN MUST BE ADDED THE EXPERIENCE OF THE SOUL.

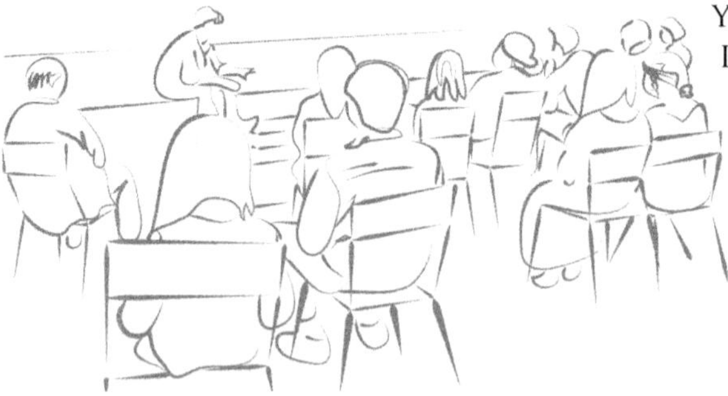

ARNOLD BENNETT
Novelist & Playwright

3

THE AWAKENING

For the redeemed, to be creative is at once to worship our Creator and to do that for which we were created.

In all honesty, I wonder if we too often miss this fact, treating our creativity cheaply at best, and at worst, working against it in ourselves and in others, responding in fear, jealousy, misunderstanding, or lack of trust. But to stifle that creativity in ourselves, or worse yet, to stifle it in someone else, is a disservice to our Creator and a continuation of the Fall. Perhaps we each have had someone in our lives who has faithfully played that role for us, inadvertently or otherwise.

My grandfather, when he was a boy, was told by one of his school teachers that he shouldn't sing because he didn't have the voice for it, and so he never sang again – until just after my youngest sister was born, at which time he sang a lullaby to her... with a voice as beautiful as an angel's. It only took one careless comment, and all that beauty and music inside him was stilled for most of his life.

Or maybe some of us do it to ourselves.

Conversely, the awakening of, the enabling and support of that creativity in a person – whether it is in yourself or someone else – is an integral part of actively building up a whole person. It is an invitation to walk daily in the Adventure that is Life in Christ. Because to live creatively is to insert ourselves intentionally into a life in which surprise, risk, and perilous courage are things to be enthusiastically pursued and savored, not evaded.

Are you going to respond to that invitation this week?

IT IS EASY TO FOLLOW,
BUT IT IS UNINTERESTING TO DO EASY THINGS.
WE FIND OUT ABOUT OURSELVES ONLY WHEN WE TAKE RISKS,
WHEN WE CHALLENGE AND QUESTION.

MAGDALENA ABAKANOWICZ
Sculptor

4

Courage

I'm always glad when I hear from artists and creative people, who, like you, are taking up the challenge of exploring their own unique, God-given creativity. As I recently mentioned to a close friend, therein lies your very own Calling. Along with it, as with every creative calling, will come great Risk and Adventure, and when pursued wholeheartedly, it will ultimately require a great deal of Courage on your part, regardless of how confident you feel about the matter.

Of course, anything that requires real Courage, by definition, also will run the risk of hitting those occasional pockets where Courage is stolen away, where it is in rare supply, where you find yourself gasping for it like oxygen at high altitudes. Where you are *dis*-Couraged.

I'll admit that I pushed through one of those breathless moments of discouragement myself just the other day, and in a strange sort of way, I'm fairly happy to be able to say that.

It's not that I enjoy the feeling of discouragement, and to be quite honest, it isn't something in which I recommend spending a whole lot of time. It's just that the folks I know who never experience discouragement are usually, though not always, the ones who avoid any situation that would require

Courage at all. Because you can't be truly dis-Couraged until you've had the occasion to have Courage in the first place. The fact that I was gasping for oxygen must mean that I was still climbing the mountain.

I know you, my dear Crazy Friend, and you are not one of those people who are content to live in what Theodore Roosevelt called that "grey twilight" where no risk is required.

And in that, you can take heart. Onward and upward…

THE BRAVE MAN IS NOT HE WHO FEELS NO FEAR,
FOR THAT WERE STUPID AND IRRATIONAL;
BUT HE, WHOSE NOBLE SOUL ITS FEAR SUBDUES,
AND BRAVELY DARES THE DANGER NATURE SHRINKS FROM.

JOANNA BAILLIE
Poet & Dramatist

5

SUCCESS AND FRUITFULNESS

I've talked to numerous truly creative people from all sorts of places who have confided in me their times of discouragement in the pursuit of their creative callings, and it so often comes down to this: that despite their earnest and extended efforts, they have yet to see Success. Very sincerely, they share with me how close they are to throwing their hands up and walking away because success has seemed so elusive. Some have even told me that Success seemed so elusive, so fantastically unattainable at the outset, that they decided not to attempt the pursuit of their Calling at all.

I suppose that, in the grand scheme of things, this is understandable. We live in a culture in which Success, as it is popularly defined, is the gold standard by which all are measured and either celebrated or found wanting. We see it as the standard in business, in government, in education, in the world of sports, entertainment, and the arts, and sadly enough, many, many times in the Church.

Oh, I don't mean that Success is an inherently bad thing – it's not. (Well, I suppose that depends on what it is we have become successful at doing…) In fact, Success is something to be thankful for when we experience it. I work towards and want to be successful as an artist and in the other areas of life. What I mean, rather, is that Success is not the measure that God intended for us to use when He called us to this adventurous life. It is not and never should be the standard by which we should measure ourselves and one another. When we do so, we set all of ourselves up for all sorts of discouragements, great and small.

That's because God never called us to be successful. He called us to be fruitful. And there's a difference. I find it interesting that in the Bible, every time that "success" is mentioned, it is in the context of "…and God gave him success," whereas He reminded His people over and over again to "be fruitful." In fact, this instruction to bear fruit was the very first command He gave after creating man and woman. The responsibility of fruitfulness was put into our hands; the responsibility of our success He kept for Himself. There are a lot of people who spend all their time struggling to learn the will of God for their lives, when they have ignored His will found in this Prime Command: *Be fruitful. Live out who I created you to be.*

Ultimately, God's command of fruitfulness is the easier one – it flows directly from what God has already loaded into us as we walk through the continuing process of Redemption. Success as a standard involves chasing a sort of "completeness" that the world set up and which it is constantly redefining. Is it any wonder that so many people live life in disheartened exhaustion? They live under the never-ending pressure to meet an ever-changing standard.

Aren't you glad that God commanded us to be fruitful, rather than to be successful? Again, please don't misunderstand me: success can be a very good thing, and in each of our Callings, we hope to see it as we proceed with hard work, perseverance, and excellence. But it isn't the ultimate measure of a man or a woman. Still, some people spend so much time worrying about being successful, they forget to be fruitful.

But when all is said and done, the opposite of failure is not success. It is fruitfulness. And that's the secret of life on the Vine.

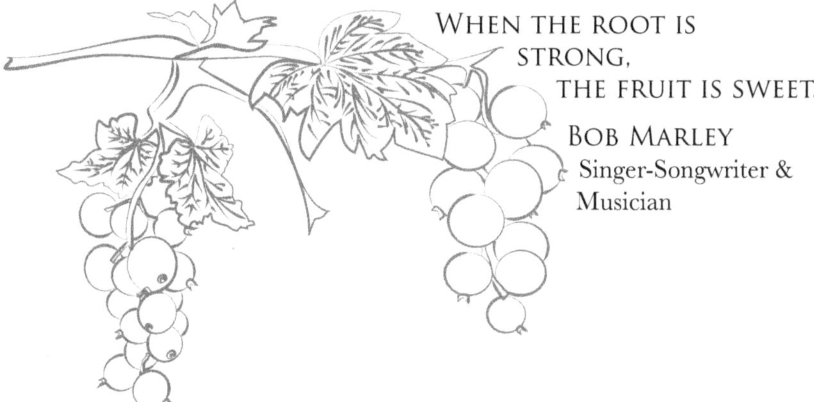

WHEN THE ROOT IS
STRONG,
THE FRUIT IS SWEET.

BOB MARLEY
Singer-Songwriter &
Musician

6

FRUITFULNESS (CONT'D)

I find it interesting, if not a bit humorous, that God's first act of creativity was to make a Garden, rather than Man and Woman, its inhabitants. No, we were not the first order of business; we were not the first to leap from God's palette. It was the Garden first. If that doesn't keep us a little humble… well, it should.

My own creative strengths, unlike my Creator's, are not in the gardening arts, however. I will readily admit – and each of the struggling plants on my balcony will attest to this – that I am not a horticulturalist. I've watered, fertilized, adjusted the amount of light, and even sweet-talked the residents of those little pots, and yet the greenery each day seems a bit browner.

My mother, on the other hand, has a way with plants. How I missed her green genes, Captain, I'll never know. And it was from her, as we both stood looking down at a pot of rapidly diminishing flowers the other day, that I learned a little secret about coaxing continuous life from these plants, a secret which, at least at first, seemed counterintuitive.

"You have to trim away the old flowers before the plant can make fresh ones," she said matter-of-factly. Somehow, eventually, that made sense. It's as if the plant is spending all its time trying to push its life into the old blooms, when that life really was meant for something fresh and new. No wonder my plants were drying up and dying: they were trying to send vitality into the old flowers, which had no business carrying life anymore, and so the new flowers could never come. And anything that doesn't bear new fruit is going to dry up pretty quickly.

I wonder if I approach my life like this a little too often – spending my time and energy trying to stuff my creative juices into the old things just because at one point they were pretty and fruitful, when in reality, God has new things to be done, fresh frontiers to be explored, new projects to be tackled, innovative ways to view the world around me. Am I willing to trim away the old, dried-up things that were fruit before, but are no longer? Am I willing to abandon them in exchange for fresh fruit? To do so will require new bursts of vision and creativity.

Ah, but therein lies my worship and my very reason to be.

I CAN'T UNDERSTAND WHY PEOPLE ARE
FRIGHTENED OF NEW IDEAS.
I'M FRIGHTENED OF THE OLD ONES.
JOHN CAGE
Composer, Philosopher & Poet

7
QUESTIONS ON MY MIND

Solely for the sake of giving you kind readers a sense of background and context, I should confess here that, before I became a professional actor and writer, I was a professional lawyer. I've found that there isn't a tremendous difference between being a trial lawyer and being an actor: both stand up in front of a group of people and tell a story, attempting to compel the people emotionally and intellectually.

There is an old adage describing each of the three years of law school: "First, they scare you to death; then, they work you to death; and finally, they bore you to death." My experience of law school provides further evidence of the truth of that description.

For those of you who haven't had the pleasure of attending law school, professors there utilize what is called "the Socratic method," named, to state the obvious, after our old pal, Socrates. The Socratic method is a Grecian formula that Socrates applied in teaching his own students, and it relies on the use of questions by the teacher to challenge students' assumptions and to guide them in critical thought toward discovery of the truth. Basically, under this method, a teacher asks a question, and the student states what he thinks the answer is. Rather than immediately agreeing or disagreeing, the teacher then continues to pose other questions that challenge his student's assumptions. At the end of this process, the student (if he is committed to intellectual honesty) will arrive at the truth – not because he is given answers, but because he is given more questions.

Socrates (and all good law professors thereafter) found that posing more questions, rather than just giving answers, is the more effective way of getting students to learn, not only because it challenges assumptions and promotes critical thinking, but because the student is receptive to the truth because he discovers it himself.

As artists, our job is similar, or at least it should be. Too many times we try to communicate some truth to our audience members by simply handing them the answer. Giving a person the right answer is useless if he doesn't know what the right question is.

So it is with art. I increasingly find that those artists who spend more time asking questions than giving answers are the ones who are most intriguing and, more often than not, lead me to discover deep truths. They challenge my intellectual and emotional assumptions. In the end, the most fascinating and enduring artists are the ones with the most fascinating and enduring questions.

One of the main reasons that some works of art, including a large majority of modern faith-based art, seem to be so lacking is that the artists who conjure up these works are so intent on giving answers that they never stop to wonder what the questions are.

Here's an example, and it's one that may rile you up at

first, unless you stop to think about it: There's an old song that asserts "Jesus is the answer for the world today…" This is a good song, but it may no longer be correct. Jesus, in fact, may not be the answer if the world today is asking the wrong questions. It would be incorrect to say that Jesus is the right answer to questions like "How do I crush my business competition?" or "How do I become wealthier than anyone else?" or "How can I become famous so I can feel significant?" – all questions the world is asking today. Jesus is not the answer to those questions, in spite of how some twist or dilute their theology to make Him so. You could put it this way: the right answer to the wrong question is the wrong answer.

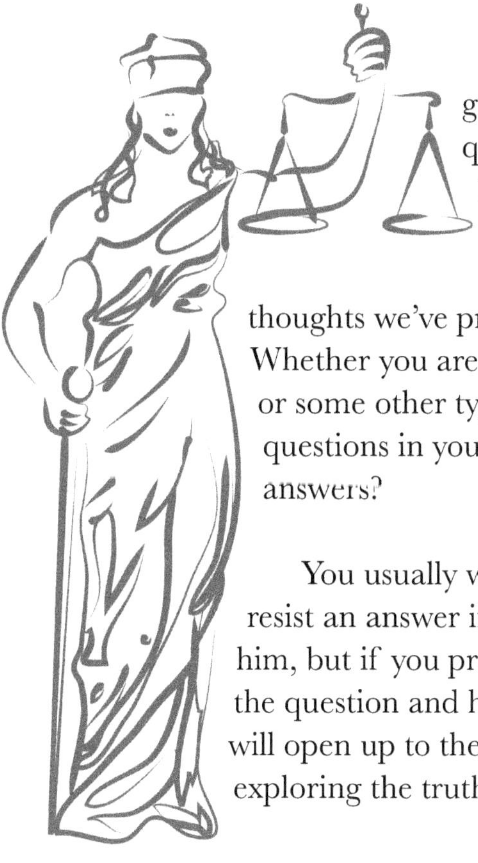

The duty of artists is to get the world to ask the right questions. We start this process by asking the right questions ourselves, questioning our assumptions, wrestling with thoughts we've previously taken for granted. Whether you are a writer, actor, filmmaker, or some other type of artist, are you asking questions in your art or are you just giving answers?

You usually will find that a person will resist an answer if you try to impose it upon him, but if you provide that same person with the question and help him to struggle with it, he will open up to the process of discovering and exploring the truth.

Here's a thought: Consider adding more questions to your creative work. For most artistic questions, the answer is to have more questions.

THE JOB OF THE ARTIST IS ALWAYS
TO DEEPEN THE MYSTERY.
FRANCIS BACON
AUTHOR, SCIENTIST & PHILOSOPHER

8

A Mild Experiment

In the days of my law practice, I would come home each night after work, and if I didn't have some social event or another to attend, I would prepare dinner and plop down in front of the television for a couple hours of cheap entertainment. Those days, I was watching a lot of crime shows, and I saw my fill of murder and mayhem just before heading off for a night of peaceful rest.

What I began to notice, however, was a bit unsettling. Each morning after an evening filled with televised violence, I would wake up with this vague sense of... *depression.*

Look, it was clear to everyone involved, including me, that these were just dramatic characterizations I was seeing on television, and I don't have a problem distinguishing fantasy from reality, at least most of the time. And I'm not really prone to being depressed; in fact, I like to think that I'm a pretty happy and fun-loving guy. So it really made me think about the impact that entertainment and media have on my life. On one hand, it saturates our environment; on the other, it was my choice to turn on the television.

"'Everything is permissible' – but not everything is beneficial. 'Everything is permissible' – but not everything is constructive," the Apostle Paul reminds us in 1 Corinthians 10.

I was talking this concept over with several people on my leadership team, and we found ourselves wondering:

> *How would we be different if we used this as our standard for the entertainment and media we consume? If we consciously decided only to take in that which is beneficial and constructive, would we be better artists?*

It is a question worth asking ourselves. How we each answer could define how dedicated we are to our respective crafts. Now I should mention that not only am I not the arbiter of what is and isn't beneficial and constructive for people in terms of entertainment, I also wouldn't want that position. And quite frankly, I still like watching crime shows on television.

But if the old adage "garbage in, garbage out" is correct, isn't the opposite also true? If we consciously decide to consume that which is beneficial and constructive – the true, the beautiful, the admirable, and all the other attributes found in Philippians 4 – doesn't that mean that the art we create will more likely be true, beautiful, and admirable?

It is not that we can't explore the darkness and its nature, but if darkness is all we explore, we will be forever blind. As a man thinks in his heart, so is he. And our art, to a large

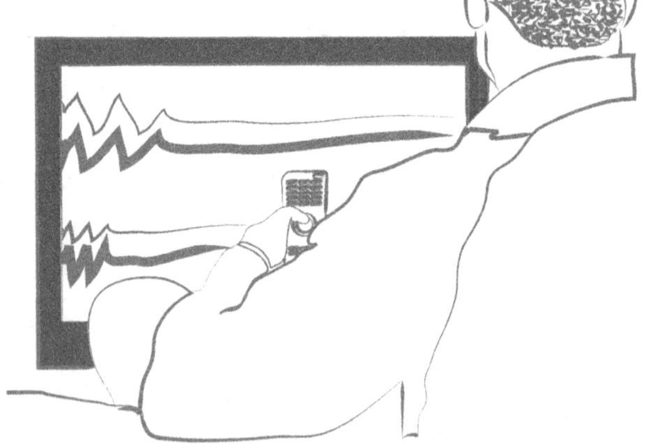

extent, comes from whom we are, or at least it does when it's effective art. Which means that our art will be a product of what we do with the ideas we take in from the entertainment and media around us.

So my leadership team is going to do a mild experiment – and you're welcome to join us if you'd like – to test this concept. For the next month, we're going to see what happens when we limit our entertainment to that which is beneficial and constructive. I anticipate that we will be better artists on the other side

ONE ALWAYS HAS TO REMEMBER THESE DAYS
WHERE THE GARBAGE PAIL IS,
BECAUSE IT'S SO EASY TO MAKE SOUNDS,
AND TO PUT SOUNDS TOGETHER INTO
SOMETHING THAT APPEARS TO BE MUSIC,
BUT IT'S JUST AS HARD AS IT ALWAYS WAS
TO MAKE GOOD MUSIC.
ROGER MOOG
Musician & Inventor

9
Seasons

Perhaps it will come as no surprise to you when I say: *I like ideas*. I like that moment of exposure to a new idea that is ripe, bursting with potential and promise. I like turning ideas over in my mind, examining them from all angles, and figuring out which ones are worthwhile to make *happen*. There is something about a new idea that makes me come alive, and I'm willing to bet that, as an artist, you're the same way. It is that moment of a great idea that keeps us energized and moving forward.

So you can imagine my dismay when, sometime in the midst of my second year as a professional artist, I sat down to go over which of my ideas were ripe for the picking and came up… empty. That had never happened before. It was a dreadful silence, much like walking into an empty auditorium, hearing only the echo of your own footsteps.

My first reaction was terror. After all, what good is an artist with no ideas? It was a momentary panic – well, more like several moments – but I managed to work my way through it with several deep breaths and a little reflection.

In the end, I was – and we all are – liberated by the words of one of our biblical poets, who reminds us in Psalm 1 that those who live in and by the life of God will "yield…

fruit in *season*." That is, we will experience a natural season for fruitfulness, which, of course, means that there will be a natural season for not bearing fruit as well. And we have to learn to embrace both seasons. Both are good and God-given, in spite of what our success-driven culture tells us.

In those moments of quiet, it's easy to look around at all the artists who are in their own seasons of happy productivity and, noting your own lack of ideas or opportunities or resources, to despair. But you must not do so; you must let the season of unfruitfulness run its course. If we refuse to allow these cyclical seasons of fruitfulness and unfruitfulness for ourselves, and instead place ourselves under the constant pressure to produce at all times, we will never permit the time to grow and develop our inner lives, and by extension, our art. In the long run, this will make our artistry rushed at best, and at worst, forced and stunted. We will end up using million-dollar words to express two-bit ideas smelling faintly of sweaty desperation.

If you are finding yourself in one of those winters of discontent, I'm happy to report from personal experience that there is always a spring around the corner. Hang on. I assure you: your fruitfulness will reappear in due season.

TO BE INTERESTED IN THE CHANGING SEASONS
IS A HAPPIER STATE OF MIND
THAN TO BE HOPELESSLY IN LOVE WITH SPRING.
GEORGE SANTAYANA
Poet & Novelist

10
Appetite for Distraction

Here's a recurring conversation I have with myself as I settle down to write each day: *Computer fired up? Check. Outline and notes handy? Check. Cup of coffee? Check. Great! I am so ready to write… and I wonder if I've gotten anything new on Facebook?*

I like to think I'm pretty diligent, but I'm often surprised by my appetite for distraction – all those little things that pull me away from the creative process. Even as I sit here writing this, there's something in the back of my mind that coolly *demands* that I surf the Internet, wander around the office, or see if something new magically has materialized in the refrigerator since the last time I looked (which was about five minutes ago) – anything *other* than what I am supposed to do: create.

What is it with such mass distraction? Those little habits – and let's be honest with ourselves: they *are* habits – typically aren't things that are intrinsically bad. In fact, usually (but not always) these little actions have a positive side to them, otherwise we wouldn't constantly be drawn back to them, and that's what keeps us justifying our indulgence in them. Yes, our pet distractions can be good, but the old quote bears repeating: Good is the enemy of Great.

The funny thing is that many of these distractions are

things that we would procrastinate over any other time – like washing dishes or cleaning the patio. But when we're supposed to be *creating*, we end up wasting our valuable creative energy and time chasing our favorite distractions. So how do you avoid doing that? Here are a few things you might give a try:

1) Make a list of the things that you know distract you. Admitting you have a problem is the first step to recovery, right? Recognize what your particular distractions are, and you'll be that much closer to avoiding them.

2) Neutralize your creative environment. If you're distracted by email, turn off the program so you don't hear that tantalizing sound for new mail. If it is a particular website, remove it from your browser's toolbar so it isn't as easy to access. Close the blinds, remove the television, silence the cell phone, kick out your office buddy – whatever it takes.

3) Make a schedule for your creative time – and stick to it. As you plan your day, set definite starting and stopping times and write them into your schedule. You can also set aside a particular amount of time for those things that distract you, so when your creative time rolls around, it's easier to remind yourself that you have another time for those activities, but at the moment, creativity is your only responsibility.

4) Begin to recognize what triggers your own temptation toward distraction. For me, it's whenever I hit the end of a plot point or a major thought as I write. In fact, I'll probably be tempted to get distracted at the end of this paragraph… but I promise to fight through it.

5) See? I made it here without getting distracted, but that leads to my next point: Be prepared for some withdrawal symptoms. Breaking the habit of distraction doesn't come easily, so at first you're going to have to work particularly hard to fight off that little voice that tells you that you deserve a break, that you *need* a break.

6) Keep a pencil and paper handy to jot down those extraneous tasks that pop into your mind. You can return to them later without fear of forgetting them.

7) Have what you need on hand before you enter your creative time: artistic supplies, a glass of water, a snack – whatever you truly need to keep yourself going.

8) Know when to take a real break, especially in those longer creative sessions. Sometimes your best inspiration comes in the middle of a good break. Just don't confuse a distraction with a break. One interrupts your creativity; the other strengthens it.

I'm sure you probably can think of a few other tips too. If so, I'd love to hear them, so drop me a note. But, please… wait until you're done your creative time.

BESIDES THE NOBLE ART OF GETTING THINGS DONE,
THERE IS THE NOBLE ART OF LEAVING THINGS UNDONE.
THE WISDOM OF LIFE CONSISTS IN THE
ELIMINATION OF NON-ESSENTIALS.

LIN YUTANG
Writer, Translator & Inventor

11

The Eyes Have It

I recently watched a wonderful film that a few friends had a hand in bringing to the silver screen. The film was well-executed, and the story was well-told, and movies with both of those elements have become way too uncommon. The premise and the plot of this particular film were so good, in fact, it all made me a bit envious. I walked out of the theater smacking myself on the forehead and wondering, *Wow, why didn't I think of that idea?*

Sometimes we miss the best creative ideas, even the ones that are sitting right in front of us, waiting to be discovered, because we don't have the eyes to see them for what they are. I suppose that is what *artistic vision* is all about, isn't it? It's the ability to see an idea with the eyes of perception and recognition.

One of my favorite passages in the Bible, and one which I think is particularly insightful for us as artists, is Isaiah 43:18-21, and especially verse 19, in which God speaks to His people:

> *See, I am doing a new thing! Now it springs up; do you not perceive it? I am making a way in the desert and streams in the wasteland.*

This declaration says a couple of things to me. First, God is still creating, and He is still doing new things. He didn't just stop being creative after six days of massive inspiration. He never gets stuck in a creative formula or rut, creating in one particular way just because that is the way it has always been done. He persists in His creative endeavors today.

Second, implicit in that verse is the warning that if we're not careful, we run the risk of not seeing and perceiving the creative things that God is doing. That is a pretty somber thought that should keep us artists on our toes, since the source of true creative inspiration starts first and foremost in and because of Him. Take note: God is the Prime Mover of creative inspiration. It starts with and flows from Him, and we want to make sure that we maintain the perception to recognize it when it springs up in front of us.

As artists, we often can find ourselves in a creative wasteland, those times when the ideas are not flowing as readily as we would like or need. But the ideas are still there; we just need the eyes to see them.

When I find myself in creative deserts like that, I take great heart in the fact that God makes streams in the wasteland. Of particular value is Jeremiah 33:3, one of the greatest promises found in the Bible for us as artists and as people:

> *Call to Me, and I will answer you, and show you great and mighty things which you do not know.*

This is a pretty amazing promise that we don't tap into often enough. It is an invitation to join God in His wonderful creativity. If we will take the time and effort to call on God, He will open our eyes to the new things He is doing.

Feeling like you've lost your creative vision somewhere in the artistic desert? Wondering if your ability to see and recognize those new ideas is forever gone? God's promise is that He will open your eyes… if you'll just call on Him.

VISION IS THE ART OF SEEING
WHAT IS INVISIBLE TO OTHERS.
JONATHAN SWIFT
Satirist, Essayist & Poet

12

The Path of Least Resistance

I've had a *Non Sequitur* comic strip on my desk for a few years entitled, "The Magic of Hollywood," in which a handful of studio executives sit around a conference table in dark business suits. The chairman of the meeting states, "A motion has been put forth that we should seek to create rather than imitate. All in favor of killing this silly notion, nod in mindless agreement…"

Unfortunately, this is what the arts and entertainment industry is too often known for.

I wonder how many times our own creativity – whether in the arts, business, or just life in general – gets shut down simply because we've spent our time imitating rather than creating. The former is usually easier than the latter, and more often than not, it's a result of neglect – failing to take the time and effort to stand up, look around, and see things in a new way, apart from what others have done or are doing. In the end, however, it's never as effective or fulfilling, artistically or otherwise.

Do we tend to do things only because "that's what's worked before" or "that's the path of least resistance" or "that's what everyone else is doing"?

It happens not only in the area of creativity, but in our broader spiritual lives as well. We have a tendency to want to take that same path of least resistance, taking our cues from those around us instead of heading out into what might be the unknown, the dangerous, or the solitary – even in those heart-thumping times we recognize that God has called us to meet Him there. This is unfortunate, especially because we are called not only to be believers in Christ, but *followers* of Christ, choosing to follow Him wherever He leads, even when that means diverging from the rest of the crowd.

NEVER FOLLOW SOMEBODY ELSE'S PATH;
IT DOESN'T WORK THE SAME WAY TWICE FOR ANYONE...
THE PATH FOLLOWS YOU AND ROLLS UP BEHIND YOU AS YOU WALK,
FORCING THE NEXT PERSON TO FIND THEIR OWN WAY.
J. MICHAEL STRACZYNSKI
Screenwriter & Producer

13

THE STORY OF GOD

Once upon a time, there was God. The Story was always about Him, although like every good story, the main character wasn't spotted in every scene. But you always knew He was there. It was His story, after all, and a fascinating story at that. Heroes rose and fell, but those who fell and were true heroes got back up again. And each one did something that no one had ever seen before and that has never been seen since.

However, like every really good story, the Story of God was filled with conflict, dark villains, and hard times. Overwhelming odds rose up. But this was to be expected, for it's impossible for anyone to have a good story without conflict. And so the Story of God became one of dark suspense, and for some, dramatic horror.

Several chapters into the Story, however, there was a sudden and unexpected plot twist (although if you look back, you can see several clues leading up to it): In the midst of those overwhelming odds, God provided a creative and unprecedented means of overcoming the odds and for infusing abundant life to all those characters who were in His story. Those characters in God's story – who were already heroes, mind you – became larger-than-life, triumphantly achieving great exploits as they battled those overwhelming odds. And so it was that with that plot twist, God's story became an action-adventure and a beautiful romance. And then…

The End.

Oh, wait, I suppose there are several letters from a few of the Story's characters (because this was a true Story), and then there's that glimpse into the eternity that is to come. All of that, we can see, is important to the telling of the tale, but then the back cover of the book is closed. We settle back with a satisfied sigh: what a good story. We laughed, we cried. Two thumbs up and a five-star rating. We remind ourselves to tell someone else the highlights of the Story. We get together weekly in a book club and discuss the Story. We commit to reading one or two chapters of the Story periodically, maybe even daily. Boy, there sure is a lot we can learn from the Story of God, now that it's completed.

But wait a minute… The audience gasps in surprise. What's this? Another plot twist! Could it be…? Yes, it is! It's almost too good to be true, but this Story, this beautiful, wonderful Story of God is not over. In spite of what some people – maybe even you – have thought, it's not completed yet.

The truth is that this is God's story, and because God has no ending, neither does His Story. His Story continues, and you and I are the ones who are writing it now. Oh, I'm not saying that we're adding to the biblical canon. What I am saying is that our lives as we live them are telling the next chapter of that Story that worked its way from Adam and Eve, through Job and Moses, Joshua and David, Esther and Elisha, and Peter, Paul and Mary. The Story continued through centuries of being written – sometimes poorly, sometimes well. And now it has come to you and me.

What will be God's story in your life? Will it be an action-adventure? A romance? Or, in spite of your best intentions, a story in which your actions and inaction are motivated by fear – that is, a horror story? Will it be a story about hesitance or courage? Will it be defined more by doctrinal correctness than by fervor, alive and growing? Will its central theme be one of waiting and wondering, or one of heroically applied faith?

Sometimes I think that, simply by default, it would be easy enough to have my chapter in this great Story end up being one of something other than great heroism and faith. But it doesn't have to be that way. It could be something tremendous. It could be something unexpected – even by all the other characters around me in the Story. It could be something no one has ever seen before. I'm pretty excited to see how it turns out. In fact, I'm excited to see how yours turns out too, and so are a lot of people – perhaps even the rest of the world. Could it be that you are the hero of your own chapter and God is waiting for you to continue His story?

MAKE VISIBLE WHAT, WITHOUT YOU,
MIGHT NEVER HAVE BEEN SEEN.
ROBERT BRESSON
Film Director

14

THE ART OF SUFFERING

At an event I spoke at several months ago, a middle-aged gentleman – let's call him Adam – pulled me aside to get some advice. He had been a professional musician for many years, especially as a guitarist, and it was his true joy and passion. However, much to his dismay, his doctor recently had told him that he was in the advanced stages of a progressive eye disorder, and that as a result, he soon was going to be completely blind.

"I don't know what I'm going to do," he said quietly. "Music is all I've done, all I've ever dreamed of doing, and now God is taking away my eyesight. Everything is going dark."

We stood there next to each other, looking at the floor. It would have been so easy for me to spit out some spiritual platitude – much too easy, I realize to my chagrin. The only thing most spiritual platitudes end up doing, whether they be in art or in relationship, is make the speaker feel smart and the recipient feel small. And usually, neither emotion is telling the truth.

We believe in a God who can heal and remove suffering in this life, but who doesn't always choose to do so. It is because God is a God of ability that a world that contains suffering is so difficult to accept. If He was not able to do anything about our suffering, if He was unable to intervene between evil and the good people who are beset by it, we could, at the very least, just shrug and get on with our lives.

But the very idea of a benevolent God who is *able* seems, at first glance, to be mutually exclusive with the existence of suffering. We are left with few options. Either God does not care about all the world's suffering, or He is not there while the world suffers, or maybe, just maybe, He has allowed that suffering to occur with some better, more valuable plan in mind.

At one point, I thought that when I became a Christian that the suffering would be over, as if by divine fiat. What I've found, however, is that the suffering isn't over; it just has taken on new meaning. Ultimately, a person who is an artist has one of the only vocations in which, when he suffers, he becomes better at what he does. (Incidentally, one of the only other such occupations is that of the pastor or minister.)

It's not that we go looking for suffering or willfully wallow in it, as some misguided artists have done. It is, however, the recognition and acceptance of the fact that when we as artists suffer or feel pain – physically, emotionally, financially, or otherwise – we have the opportunity to become deeper and richer and less willing to rely on cheap answers.

It is no coincidence that cultures that have experienced the deepest suffering and persecution have also produced some of the most compelling art. It is the same for us as individuals; the pain prompts us to struggle, to sweat, to drag out the unwilling answers for the difficult and otherwise overlooked questions that accumulate in our souls through the season of suffering. And our art can reflect all of that – if we will allow it to do so.

It is then that we become truly passionate artists, realizing that the very word *passion* is derived from the Latin *passio*, which means "suffering."

All I found myself able to do with Adam that evening was to stand with him as a fellow artist. I reminded him of certain artists – Beethoven, Van Gogh, Ray Charles, and Stevie Wonder – whose work became something greater not in spite of, but *because* of their suffering. I reminded him of the role that pain and suffering have in the life of the artist who is willing to accept and embrace it. I put my hand on his shoulder and prayed to the God who longs to heal and who doesn't always do so.

IT'S A BEAUTIFUL THING TO SEE THROUGH THE EYES
OF PAIN AND HEARTACHE STRAIGHT INTO THE NIGHT
WE RUN FROM THE DARKNESS OF THIS LIFE
BUT IF WE'LL TURN AROUND, WE'LL FIND A LITTLE BIT OF LIGHT.
PHIL KEAGGY
Guitarist & Vocalist

15

SEARCHING FOR SIGNIFICANCE

I've got a good friend who is a successful writer for television sitcoms. At an event one evening, a woman approached him and asked, "How can I help my young daughter to become a successful Hollywood writer?" In his characteristic wit doused in friendly sarcasm, my friend replied: "Withhold your love from her for the next ten years."

One of the main reasons many creative people come to Hollywood – and this is at the same time rarely mentioned and rarely denied – is that they are looking for significance, a sense of actually mattering in and to this world. I'm sure that we could summon up a swarm of psychologists who would agree, asserting that many creative people, and especially performers, are driven by a need to fill the hole left by not feeling love or significance in their formative years – perhaps even from a mother or father, as my writer friend suggested.

And without going too far into the depths of modern psychology, it actually may be true. The search for the feeling of significance often motivates us artistic folks to perform – in our writing, our acting, our filmmaking, or whatever it is that we do creatively. That can even, at times, lead to noteworthy accomplishments in our artistic pursuits.

With that said, it's important to keep in mind that it's not our talents or abilities that actually make us significant in this life. To fall into the trap of thinking otherwise may or may not allow us to succeed in the world of creativity, but it will certainly leave us continuously chasing after a further sense of meaning. And that's because the feeling of significance – like all emotions – comes and goes, and eventually fades away.

Ultimately, a significance that fades away is, in the grand scheme of things, insignificant. If we as humans and artists truly have significance, if we truly have meaning – and I'm convinced that we do – it's because of something, or someone, much more abiding and permanent than any emotion we could have about ourselves.

One of the great schemes of the Devil, in all his artful cunning, is to convince us to chase after that which we already have in abundance. So it is with significance: We already have more of it than we know how to wield, and yet our wholehearted pursuit of it drives us toward all sorts of achievement and folly.

I will suggest here, and you're free to provide evidence to the contrary if you're able, that you will not become more significant by selling that script you're writing, or landing that lead role, or directing a feature film, or any other artistic accomplishment that delivers applause or celebrity.

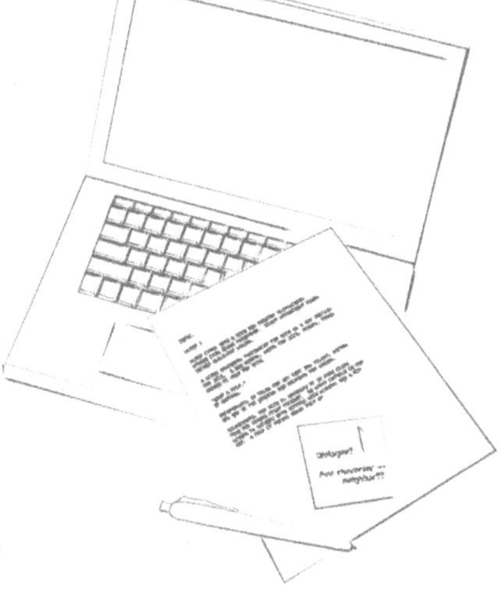

When it comes down to it, we must remember this: We don't have significance because we are artistic; we are artistic because we have significance. The spotlight does not bring more significance; it only illuminates what is already there.

If we can grasp that fact, it will change who we are as people and why we do what we do as artists.

THE AIM OF ART IS TO REPRESENT NOT
THE OUTWARD APPEARANCE OF THINGS,
BUT THEIR INWARD SIGNIFICANCE.
ARISTOTLE
Writer & Philosopher

16

Take A Message

Last week, I received a gracious invitation to attend the high school graduation ceremony for Amy, the sister of a friend of mine. It truly was an honor to be invited, but I'll be honest: graduation ceremonies are not high on my list of enjoyable activities, including the various times I had to march across the stage to receive my own hard-earned sheepskins. In my opinion, such ceremonies tend to be long, hot, and overly orchestrated.

Lest it sound like I protest too much, however, let me state that every once in a while, there escapes from the confines of all that gratuitous pomp and circumstance a moment of truth and beauty that strikes me and sticks. In the case of Amy's graduation, it came in the form of an interaction she had with her former third grade teacher, who handed Amy a beautiful card congratulating her on her achievements. At the end of the brief note, and just above her shaky signature, this teacher wrote one final lesson to her erstwhile student: *Don't forget: your life is your message.*

I've been mulling over that simple admonition ever since Amy read it out loud to us. *Your life is your message.* Those five words say more than we realize at first glance.

According to the history books, Hollywood producer

Samuel Goldwyn wasn't too interested in sending messages through art. Legend has it that, when challenged to do so in his films, he retorted, "If you want to send a message, call Western Union," or words to that effect.

Most creative artists I meet, however, don't agree with Goldwyn's witticism. Most artists – including me – *want* to say something meaningful with the art they create, as if to do otherwise somehow cheapens what they are working so hard to fashion *ex nihilo*. It's not that the art exists solely for the purpose of delivering the message – this would justify art only as a means to an end, and good art needs no such justification (a fact too often overlooked or denied by many faith-based artists). Be that as it may, when it comes down to it, most artists want their works to say something, to speak to the ages, even if it is just a message from the soul.

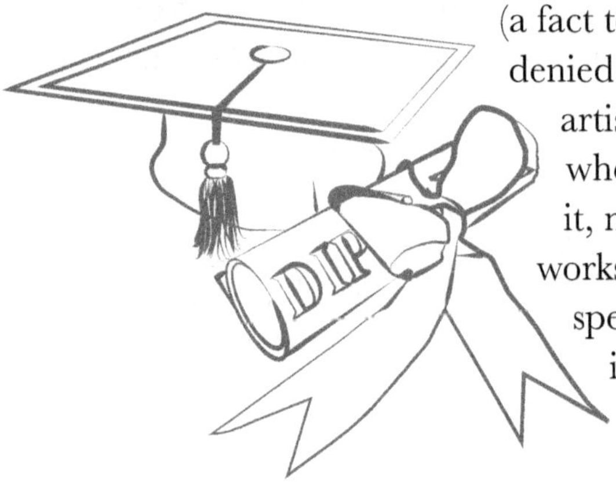

And we get frustrated if our intended message does not come through in our art to the world around us, and rightly so. Nothing is worse for an artist than when he tries to say something true and beautiful through his art and his art doesn't comply.

It comes as no surprise that we feel this way as creative artists. After all, our Creator, in whose likeness we were formed, also intended to send a message through His artwork – that is to say, us. *For we are God's workmanship, created in Christ Jesus to do good works…* (Ephesians 2:10a). And He has something He wants to communicate to a weary world through you, a message that is yours and yours alone to embody. It must be frustrating to Him any time He tries to say something true and beautiful through His art and His art doesn't comply.

You put a lot of care into your craft. Do you do the same with the life you lead? What is communicated each day as you live and breathe, in private and in public and in performance? By the words you use, the actions you take, the relationships you have? By the changes you bring to the world?

All of this is worthy of that same artistic regard. After all, your life is your message.

NOT ONLY MUST THE MESSAGE BE CORRECTLY DELIVERED,
BUT THE MESSENGER HIMSELF MUST BE SUCH
AS TO RECOMMEND IT TO ACCEPTANCE.
J.B. LIGHTFOOT
Writer & Theologian

17

The Art of Grace

I'm slowly beginning to find that I enjoy the artful practice of grace here in this culture so much more than those times I am only asserting my theological "rightness." The art of grace does something in the person to whom it is directed, it does something in the world around us – and like all good art – it does something in the artist practicing it. Far from being a limp, inactive, or wishy-washy concept of merely letting wrongs slide, I'm starting to discover that real grace is proactive, effective, full of muscle and potency. Perhaps that is why the Apostle Paul called Timothy to be "strong in the grace."

Please don't misunderstand me: there have been times in Hollywood and the arts & entertainment world when I've been called to stand up and speak the truth in the face of a wrong or an evil, and I'm sure that there will be more times like that in the future. I want, in all such cases, to rise to the challenge without flinching. But in those moments, I hope to be more like Tuesday's child from the old poem – "full of grace."

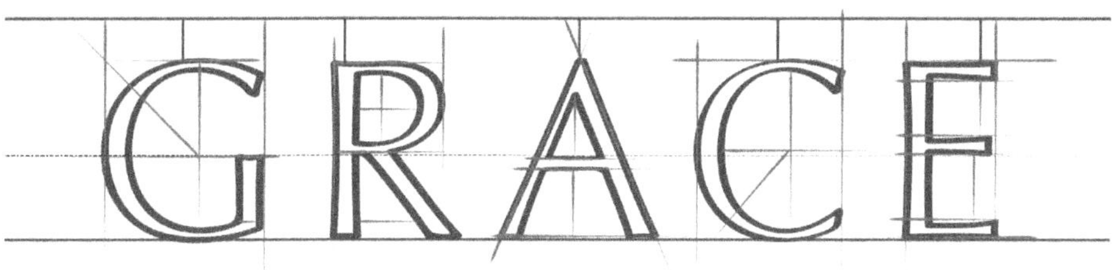

How interesting that it was not Sunday's child – perhaps that's because we are called out into the middle of the week to exhibit the full expression of this grace. Among those who need it the most.

And that includes me.

GRACE, IT'S THE NAME FOR A GIRL
IT'S ALSO A THOUGHT THAT CHANGED THE WORLD...
SHE CARRIES A PEARL IN PERFECT CONDITION
WHAT ONCE WAS HURT, WHAT ONCE WAS FRICTION
WHAT LEFT A MARK NO LONGER STINGS
BECAUSE GRACE MAKES BEAUTY OUT OF UGLY THINGS.

BONO
Singer and Musician

18

Exploring the Mystery

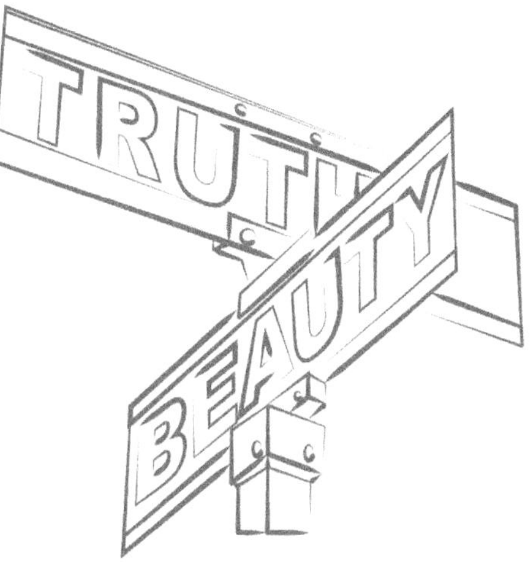

There's a thought that's been nagging at me for some time now, and that is this: It is important to remind ourselves that there is an aspect of being an artist that goes beyond simply giving answers to people. The artistic voice is a prophetic one, or at least it was meant to be, in that its purpose is to communicate Truth and Beauty, even in – and maybe *especially* in – circumstances that are adverse or antagonistic to them.

A fallacy that artists and prophets can far too easily buy into is that, because we are the communicators of Truth and Beauty in our culture, we are also the authority on Truth and Beauty. That is far from the case, and it's a dangerous mistake, because it leads to the incorrect assumption that, contained in our brains, so wonderful and so finite, are all the answers the world needs.

This is a fatal error for an artist because it results in the artist ceasing to recognize that there is much more out there than he or she already knows, which leads to a gradual failure to explore beyond the answers already accumulated, which ultimately leads to a loss of wonder.

It is wonder, this sense that there is a world bigger than we know, that makes artistry worthwhile as a continuous pursuit. It takes humility to admit that there are things we don't yet understand. But those who believe they already have all the answers and who approach their art from that standpoint end up missing so much. They miss all the wonder and awe that is essential to their craft. The calling of creative artists is to explore the mystery and to communicate it, unencumbered by over-simplified answers, to a world that has lost its wonder.

The same is true of us as believers as we explore the Source of that mystery. We must not get so focused on the aspects of God we *do* understand that we fail to worship the aspects we *don't*. I must allow all of God to live inside of me – both the parts that I understand as well as the parts that remain a mystery. All of these aspects are Truth and Beauty, whether I understand them or not.

It is either all or none. It is either an invitation to the God of both revelation and mystery to make His home in me, His handiwork, or it is to rely on my own limited understanding and create a god of my own choosing, a god who becomes my handiwork. Since the very essence of God will not – *cannot* – be limited by my finite understanding, the latter is really not an option worth considering.

The depth of our faith and artistry is determined by how we relate and respond to Truth and Beauty – both that which is known and that which is unknown. So take a

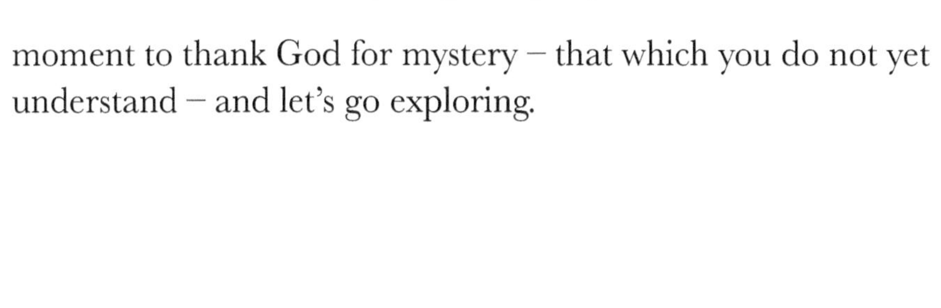

moment to thank God for mystery – that which you do not yet understand – and let's go exploring.

THE MOST BEAUTIFUL THING WE CAN EXPERIENCE IS THE MYSTERIOUS. IT IS THE SOURCE OF ALL TRUE ART AND SCIENCE. HE TO WHOM THE EMOTION IS A STRANGER, WHO CAN NO LONGER PAUSE TO WONDER AND STAND WRAPPED IN AWE, IS AS GOOD AS DEAD: HIS EYES ARE CLOSED.

ALBERT EINSTEIN
Theoretical Physicist

19

An Open Letter To a Crazy Friend

Dear Crazy Friend,

You and I have known each other for some time now, and in all our conversations, which I have valued so much, you swear up and down to me that you are not a creative person, or at best, that your creativity is sadly lacking. And I just as earnestly tell you that you are sadly mistaken. You see creativity as a gift of the chosen few, much like some folks who are blessed with the ability to curl their tongues into a circle or others who can eat large amounts of ice cream (I'm talking about the real stuff, mind you, not frozen yogurt or that dubious "ice milk") and never gain weight.

As if those who are creative are not only in a class of their own, but apparently in their own genus and species as well.

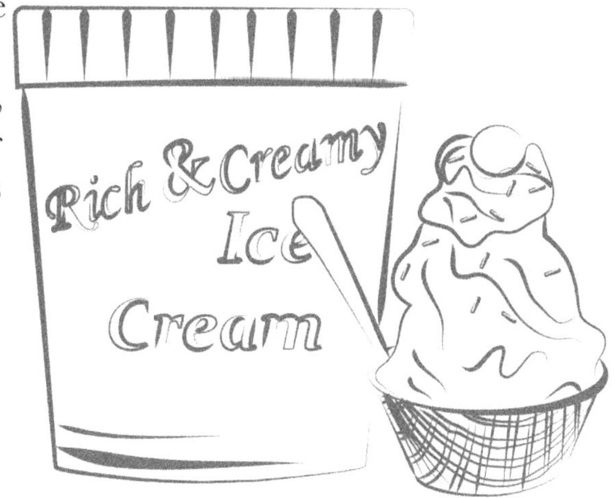

Now, don't get me wrong. Each time I sit down with you for a heart-to-heart conversation about creativity, art, and the adventurous life, we see things pretty much eye-to-eye. But for some reason, I've yet to get through to you on this one crucial topic – that of your own inherent creativity – no matter how logical I make it for you. Let me try again here:

a) God is creative, as demonstrated by the fact that His first recorded actions were those of tremendous creative artistry; and

b) God created each of us in His own image; *ergo*

c) Each one of us is creative.

Though simple, this is far from being merely a silly syllogism. In fact, it goes much deeper than we can know. Creativity is at the core of who and what we were created to be. We were created to be creative. To do new things, to expand our horizons. True, that creativity may come through in a variety of ways; you have your ways, and I have mine. One woman I know is forever coming up with exciting new business ideas and structures; another is incredibly adept at developing beautiful interior designs. I know a guy who is always developing new ways of connecting people. Each is an artist in his or her own way and medium. Oddly enough, I even know a lawyer or two whose creativity is best expressed in the legal practice.

Here in Hollywood, we are surrounded by writers and poets, musicians and filmmakers, actors and orators. Creativity is the field in which we all exercise our freedom in Christ. By the Fall, that creativity was stilted or stilled, but through the Redemption, it is revived and released. It is that Redemption that is an invitation to the adventure of your creativity.

Your creative life calls, my dear Crazy Friend, and so does mine... Shall we, then?

Your Crazy Friend,
Shun Lee

A TRULY CREATIVE PERSON RIDS HIM OR HERSELF OF ALL SELF-IMPOSED LIMITATIONS.
GERALD JAMPOLSKY
Writer & Psychiatrist

20
The Sound of Your Voice

Shortly after I joined the Screen Actors Guild, a friend and I attended one of the Guild's seminars on a topic that is near and dear to every artist's heart: health insurance. Now, that isn't the most stimulating topic, so in order to keep from nodding off, I found myself looking around at the other people in the room. Perhaps it was my brain attempting to amuse itself, but I found myself suppressing a grin as I saw various people in the room who looked just like certain celebrity actors.

Down the row to my left was someone who looked almost exactly like a well-known lead actor. Off to my right was an actress who looked like a prominent sitcom star. And as I waited in line to ask a question after the seminar was finished (a sure sign I hadn't been listening well), I ran into a guy who I'm pretty sure had fashioned himself after Robert Redford, circa, ironically enough, *The Natural*, even down to the same hairstyle and smile.

I should state right off the bat that each of these people appeared to be earnest and well-meaning, and the one who I talked to was actually a very nice person. But it all got me wondering whether the most that any of these actors would achieve would be to copy the original. It's not that an artist can't imitate – in fact, some have made a decent living out of the practice. There is definitely a good place for mimicry, satire, parody, and caricature. But if an actor's job is to imitate life, were these actors going to end up sort of one step removed? Actors imitating actors who imitate life? So it got me thinking about what life is like when it is spent in imitation.

It has been said that imitation is the sincerest form of flattery. I suppose that could be true. But I wonder if a person who only copies what has been done before, a person who fails to find his or her own voice, is truly living out who he or she is meant to be as an artist. If you are truly the artwork of God – and I believe you are – then there is something unique and different that He wants to say through you if you're willing to do so. We each have a perspective that is completely original, and it is from there that our art should come. To spend our artistic lives only imitating others and what has been done before is to mute the artistic voice that God has given each of us.

What keeps us from being an original, from taking the time to discover our own artistic voice? It can be any number of reasons: fear of what other people will think, fear of what the Church will think, fear that our art won't be accepted, fear of failure, fear of success. But none of these are good reasons, are they? I've said it before: fear is never a good reason for doing anything.

Ask yourself this as you go about your artistic craft this week: *Have you found your own voice? And if not, what's keeping you from discovering and sharing it?*

The world is waiting for something original, and believe it or not, you are it.

THE WHOLE POINT IN DEVELOPING YOUR OWN STYLE
IS TO FIND YOUR OWN VOICE.
DAVE HOLLAND
Jazz Bassist, Composer & Bandleader

21

The Greatest of Ease

At the beginning of this year, I started taking lessons in a Chinese martial arts form called Wing Chun. My *sifu* (or teacher) is my good friend, Brian, who is a man of many talents – among other things, he is an artist and an author, a pastor, a college professor, and a double black belt in wing chun.

I've been working on a film project that will require some martial arts for my role, and Brian very generously stepped in to help with the fight choreography and to whip me into shape. I'd always wanted to learn some martial arts. I think that maybe a part of that has to do with my genetic disposition, but if I'm to be truly honest with you, mostly it's because, and I say this with all seriousness, it looks really cool. The precision, the balance, the fluidity of motion. When done well, kung fu is – like dance – poetry in motion.

I've seen a lot of martial arts movies over the years, going back to when I was just a little kid. At that age, those films left me 1) full of hyperactivity, and 2) with the same thought that washed over me any time I watched a film with one of my many heroes – Superman, Indiana Jones, Luke Skywalker, Robin Hood, or Rocky the Flying Squirrel – and that thought was an enthusiastic *Hey! I could do that!*

It was enough to fill me with aspiration and my mother with terror. Having on her hands an easily inspired son with a penchant for pointed projectiles and free flight, she learned quickly to limit my viewing habits.

Unfortunately, watching kung fu and doing kung fu are two very different things, requiring two very different sets of abilities, a fact that I'm learning under Brian's patient guidance now. I'm coming along slowly but surely, but I've got quite a bit more practice ahead of me before I can say that I'm proficient.

It's that way with everything in life, however, and it is especially true in the creative arts, whether it is acting, writing, film, painting, dance, music or any of the other art forms. It can look pretty easy while we are watching it, but when we try our own hands at it, we find that easy has nothing to do with it.

That's because all the things that are worthwhile – artistry, creativity, and faith, to name but a few – require focus, passion, persistence, attention to details, dedication to the craft, and practice, practice, practice. Talent, that wonderful asset that you and I both possess in our own ways, is only the beginning; talent is a blunt instrument that can be wielded clumsily or with finesse, depending on the amount of time, effort, and dedication the practitioner has spent with it.

Whatever your particular craft is, whether it is acting or dance or writing or kung fu, what will make you impressive is not that it is something that is done with ease. Rather, what will make you impressive is that you have undertaken something difficult and somehow made it look easy. And before you can reach the point of doing so, much like with my kung fu, you will have to stretch yourself, fall down a lot, and even take it on the chin a few times.

So as I sit here gingerly tending the large bruise on my forearm from yesterday's workout, I'm reminded of this fact:

Good art, like any act of faith, does not come easily. The very fact that it is difficult is what, at least in part, makes it worthwhile. It would be a mistake to think otherwise.

WHAT WE HOPE TO DO WITH EASE,
WE MUST FIRST LEARN TO DO WITH DILIGENCE.
SAMUEL JOHNSON
Author & Poet

22

Letter To a Crazy Friend: The Fine Art of Friendship

My Dear Crazy Friend,

It was, as it always is when I receive personal mail from a good friend, a terrific pleasure to receive your letter the other day. In today's hurried world, a handwritten letter arriving in a mailbox seems to be one of those increasingly rare gestures by which one person stops, thinks, and transcends the urgent pace of daily living. And in the process, actually *connects* with another person.

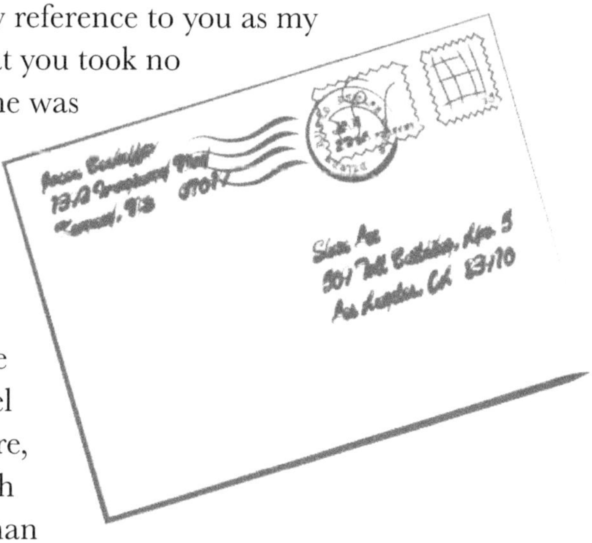

But enough of such slice-of-life musings. I'm glad that you found the humor in my reference to you as my "crazy" friend, and that you took no offense. Of course, none was intended. Far from it, in fact. The longer that I walk through this weary world, the more I am impressed by and drawn to people who are willing to travel off the beaten path. Sure, some may consider such nonconformity more than just a little nuts, but as I have been reminded repeatedly by other friends and bright legal minds from places as far away as Washington, Minnesota, Florida, Texas, and yes, Virginia, there is no sanity clause when it comes to the contract of friendship, even in this skeptical age. And for my own part, I've been entirely grateful for that fact on more than one occasion.

We are involved in a culture in which true friends are uncommon, and maybe even more so in the entertainment industry. In show business, there is the suspicion that any extension of friendship is just part of the show. There is often – maybe always – that thought that resides in the back of our brains, *"What does this person want from me?"* This industrial distrust of our fellow creative artists is at once both warranted and harmful to us individually and as a community. It is one of the reasons I urge artists to learn first to serve others with their creative talents rather than serving themselves. I've been assured that this philosophy will get me laughed out of the entertainment industry, and maybe it will, but at least it will allow me to retain my humanity.

Who are your true friends? And how do you know when you are truly being a friend? Along with the importance of learning to lay down all that we are and can be for someone else, let me suggest to you that one of the most vital traits found in true friendship is "speaking the truth in love" to one another. Truth and love. One without the other is not friendship. The people who are eager to speak the truth but are lacking in love are only abrasive. The people who are full of love but never speak up with the truth are softly ineffective. Truth *and* love. If you would be a friend, both are required of you.

The old axiom in show biz is true: it is indeed all about who you know. The question that we each must ask ourselves, therefore, and especially as artists, is this: *Are we being friends to those who we know?*

The answer to this question has deeper implications than we often realize. Because it is the fine art of friendship that will transform this world of the arts.

Your Crazy Friend,
Shun Lee

PERHAPS THE MOST DELIGHTFUL FRIENDSHIPS ARE THOSE IN WHICH THERE IS MUCH AGREEMENT, MUCH DISPUTATION, AND YET MORE PERSONAL LIKING.

GEORGE ELIOT
Novelist & Poet

23

TRUTH AND LOVE, REVISITED

The following is an actual letter I received at The Greenhouse offices in response to the previous essay:

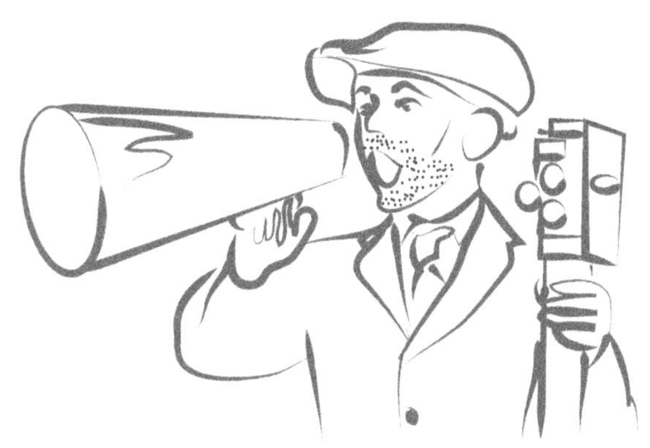

Dear Shun Lee,

You wrote in your last essay that, "The people who are eager to speak the truth but are lacking in love are only abrasive. The people who are full of love but never speak up with the truth are softly ineffective. Truth and love. If you would be a friend, both are required of you." You also mentioned, "The old axiom in show biz is true: it is indeed all about who you know. The question that we each must ask ourselves, therefore, and especially as artists, is this: Are we are being friends to those who we know?"

I spoke the truth to a first-time director who repeatedly refused to give direction, and instead of listening, he fired me. Regardless of how he responded to me, was I the true friend to confront him? Should I have been gentler and more loving?

Sincerely,
A Cinematographer

Dear Cinematographer,

Thanks for the email. Those are very good questions. I'd be happy to give a few thoughts.

We'll never be able to predict how some people will respond to the truth, even when spoken in love. In fact, the Bible tells us not to be surprised when we are mistreated for doing what is right. Unfortunately, we're dealing with (and are ourselves) broken people who carry the wounds that life in a fallen world so often inflicts. This means that speaking the truth in love isn't a formula for achieving the results we want; it is, rather, the way we are directed to live, behave, and carry ourselves. Even in response to being fired, we then are able to say, "I may not have kept the job, but I did behave in a way that pleased God." Ultimately, being able to say that is *always* better than any job, no matter how big, small, or important to our career that job may be.

My other thought is that an important part of the love aspect of "speaking the truth in love" is what I will call the "time, place, and manner" of truth-telling. That is to say that in speaking the truth to somebody, love requires choosing wisely *when* we speak the truth, *where* we speak the truth, and *how* we speak the truth (for example, our tone, our word choices, whether we insist on our own way, the degree of professionalism we display, etc.). Without knowing how your specific situation went down, I can't comment on how you approached it. But if you suspect that you should have been gentler or more loving in your exchange with the director, that may be something you can address, perhaps even in following up with the director.

That's not to say that the truth spoken in love will always be gentle. Jesus certainly spoke the truth in love as He angrily flipped the moneychangers' tables in the temple, and that doesn't appear to have been gentle. The difference between what He did there and what we too often do, is that in the midst of all the table-turning, Jesus knew He would be laying down his life in a few hours for those same moneychangers – and then He went out and did it. And that is love. In our every relationship, our every conversation, our every exchange, may we go and do likewise.

All my best,
Shun Lee

A TRUTH THAT'S TOLD WITH BAD INTENT
BEATS ALL THE LIES YOU CAN INVENT.
WILLIAM BLAKE
Poet, Painter & Printmaker

24

THE QUICK AND THE DEAD

One of the most wearisome parts of being human is the amount of time that it can take to get anywhere, especially the places you *want* to go. It can be oh-so-difficult to have a God-given vision of what should be, of what could be, of what exists so clearly in one's imagination and faith – and yet have it just out of reach for what seems to be an interminable amount of time. The desire to see the vision materialize into existence may prompt an individual to keep working toward the goal, but for some reason that same desire almost never makes the goal arrive any sooner than it is supposed to.

I've had the opportunity to learn that lesson over and over again, and find it at work even as an artist. Maybe *especially* as an artist. It's just that I can see the goal so clearly. It's inspiring! It's pristine! It's glorious! I can point it out to the people who are going there with me and describe it to those who are encouraging me along the way. But aside from diligently plodding along, putting one foot in front of the other, I can't seem to make the trip go any *faster*.

Apparently, that isn't up to me, no matter how much I pick up the pace.

That is the irony of our respective journeys – we have stewardship over the process of the journey to the destination, but it seems that we have little, if any, control over how long that journey is going to take. On second thought, scratch that. I should say that, by all appearances, we have plenty of ability to *hamper* things on our own – by our distractions, our indecisions, our over-analysis, and our hesitations, all of which we seem to have in abundance – but we don't seem to be able to arrive at our destinations before their time.

To everything, according to one songwriter, there is a season, and just to add to the angst, a completely different songwriter assures us that the waiting is the hardest part. Perhaps this comes from a fear of being late, even though the promise is that all things will be made beautiful in their own time. And so we find ourselves cursing the slowness by which we head towards our goals.

A couple years ago, I found myself in a place in life in which I couldn't drive my car for several months. In the vast sprawl that is Los Angeles, getting very far was nothing short of frustrating. So a generous friend bought me a good bicycle. It was a terrific blessing, and one for which I was truly grateful (you who did it, you know who you are) – and for more than one reason. Yes, it got me where I needed to go, and sure, it got me in pretty good shape, but that bike helped me to do something even more substantial and worthwhile. It got me to *slow down.*

Suddenly (if I can use that word in the context of 'slowing down'), I was traveling not at the breakneck speed of the typical Southern California automobile driver, but at the pace of the urban bicyclist. No longer able to use the freeway system, I was forced to find alternate routes, side streets, and hidden neighborhoods that I never would have sought out if I were in a car. And the strange thing I came to realize was that, in spite of my slower pace, I was *enjoying* myself. I could catch the smell of spices as I passed through various ethnic neighborhoods. I received a smile and a wave from the mother and her little girl playing in their tiny yard. I could hear neighbors chatting with each other over fences. I could see the small mom-and-pop shops and the wares they displayed in their windows. I could read clever graffiti on the sides of buildings (well… *some* of it was clever).

And all these were things that I never would have had the opportunity to experience if I had been going as fast as I wanted to. All of a sudden, the world was bigger because I was going slowly enough to see the small details. And so, oddly enough, I was thankful for this pace, which I would have otherwise considered sluggish, because it left me with a sensation that I was increasingly… *alive*.

I felt sorry for all those motorists who were unaware of this breathing world that existed at the slower tempos. I felt sorry for those drivers who had their feet clamped down on their accelerators and who couldn't be engaged in all the life that was going on around them. I pitied the quick and the dead.

These days, I'm back in the driver's seat of my 1995 Toyota Camry, hoping that perhaps someday a generous friend will buy me a better, faster car (you who are supposed to do it, you know who you are). My right foot is clamped down on the accelerator in my effort to keep up with the speed demons of the freeway. In the midst of the frenzy, however, I'm haunted by spices and chatter and clever graffiti and a thought that slowly takes shape in my mind like all those goals and destinations I can envision so clearly, and that thought is this:

Faster is not always better.

SLOW DOWN AND ENJOY LIFE.
IT'S NOT ONLY THE SCENERY YOU MISS BY GOING TOO FAST—
YOU ALSO MISS THE SENSE OF WHERE YOU ARE GOING AND WHY.
EDDIE CANTOR
Comedian, Singer & Actor

25
Wrestling With God

Dear Shun Lee,

I was wondering if you ever felt that writing pulled you away from God. Sometimes I feel that way. I'm not sure if my faith is just weak in that area. I may need therapy.

Sincerely,
A Writer From Florida

Dear Writer From Florida,

Remember that art is and should be about wrestling with God, not just reciting truths. In fact, the Apostle Paul talks about how we, when we became Christians, were grafted into the vine of Israel—and the name "Israel" means "he who wrestles with God." The pull and push that is wrestling with God is a large part of what our relationship should be with Him.

At times your art, when properly done, will lead you into places in which you will have to wrestle with God to find His deeper truths. At times, that will feel like you are pulling away from Him. But the very fact that you're concerned that you might be pulling away shows that you have a relationship with Him and recognize His centrality in the whole difficult mess of writing. And it should be a difficult mess—if it were not, then I would question whether you are really doing it correctly.

Allow me to offer you this quote by Bono, who is the lead singer of the rock band U2 and who examines this question in the context of music, which, as you know, is just writing set to melody and harmony: *The music that really turns me on is either running toward God or away from God. Both recognize the pivot, that God is at the center of the jaunt.*

And just like Jacob, in the process of wrestling with God, expect to come away with a limp in the sinews of what you thought was such solid truth—a recognition that the strength you so confidently relied upon to stand had to be impaired in order to show you who you really are in relationship with Him.

You said it correctly: Your faith is weak, and so is mine. That is what we mourn as part of the human condition, as part of our fallenness. And so, in His kindness, God gives us our therapy, which is our art.

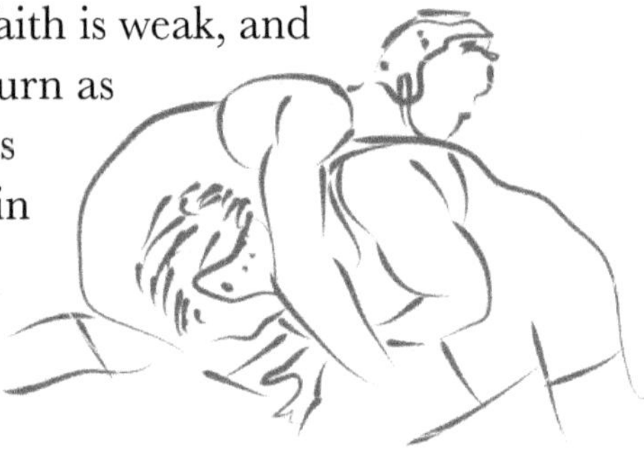

All my best,
Shun Lee

A WORK OF ART IS THE TRACE OF A MAGNIFICENT STRUGGLE.
GRACE HARTIGAN
Artist & Painter

26

Beyond Belief

A couple weeks ago, I went on a personal retreat in Palm Springs. I have some good friends who donated their timeshare condo for me to use, which, of course, made them even better friends. I say that tongue-in-cheek. After all, I was in the middle of the desert by myself, and real friends don't do that to friends, right? I'm kidding. In all fairness, they did offer to come along, but sensing that God had a few things to say to me, I went out alone into the wilderness to pray and listen.

Wandering in the desert for a few days got me thinking about the Israelites, who ended up wandering in the desert for a few years. I know there are a lot of creative artists in the entertainment industry and elsewhere who sometimes get the feeling that they've been wandering in a desert for days, weeks, or even years at a time. I've been there too.

There are many reasons why a person might end up in the desert, so if you find yourself there, I'll leave it to God to reveal why that may be. After all, some desert times are God-ordained. Jesus, Paul, David, and other great heroes spent a lot of their formative years out in the wilderness.

Other desert times are not part of God's preferred agenda, however. The Israelites spent a good, long time wandering in the desert, not so much because of their complaining – which some people mistakenly think was the catalyst – but because of their *unbelief. (Heb. 3:19)*.

Why, after all of Egypt, must there be a desert? The desert is less a punishment, and more a refinement. The fire and the heat give rise to hidden unrighteousness so we can deal with it. In Israel's case, the desert showed the unbelief that apparently came pretty naturally to them at the time.

Unbelief prevents you from entering into God's promises for you. In Israel's case, it kept them from entering the Promised Land. It wasn't that the Israelites didn't believe in God or the spiritual world. They did. What they didn't believe in was God's character. Their unbelief was directed towards His ability and desire to fulfill His promises. They allowed their immediate circumstances and abilities to dictate their belief, rather than God's character and the relationship He promised to them.

Oh, there were a couple guys who didn't fall into that sin of unbelief (and yeah, I'm sorry to say, it *is* sin). Joshua and Caleb were the only two among all the Israelites who were allowed to enter into God's promises because they believed that His character, favor, and ability trumped everything else. *That* was belief in God.

In your artistic life, you may have encountered setbacks and difficult circumstances. As a result, you may have let unbelief creep into your thinking, maybe without even realizing it. I know, I know – some truly rotten things may have happened to you. But a reason for sin is not the same as an excuse for sin. No, I get it – you still believe in God's existence. But do you still believe in His character?

Belief is not a tool; it is a position. It is positioning yourself to receive from the Father whatever He wants to give. It is a choice to agree that He exists and to agree with what He says is true about His character and what your relationship is with Him. It is not a tool to get what you want, but a position you place yourself in to receive what He gives. It is openness; it is receptivity.

Belief is a muscle. It becomes stronger, with more stamina, each time you choose to use it. Failure to use it, however, leads to atrophy. So if you find yourself wandering in the desert, check your belief levels. Move beyond belief in your surroundings and your own abilities to belief in the character of God.

LIVE YOUR BELIEFS AND YOU CAN TURN THE WORLD AROUND.
HENRY DAVID THOREAU
Author, Philosopher & Poet

27

THE BACKGROUND

In my first few months in Hollywood, I spent some time in one of the more anticlimactic positions in the entertainment industry, that of the Background Actor. I know you've seen them: those seemingly inconsequential people tucked into the corners of film and television scenes, sitting in the coffee shop or walking intently by or engaging in earnest (but silent) conversations or doing whatever it is they've been directed to do. In those rare moments you pay any attention to them at all, it's usually only to wonder, briefly and rather indifferently, what they're talking about, before you turn your attention back to the lead characters.

Being in the background is not always easy work. Several years ago, the last television scene in which I was an extra, although shot here in Los Angeles, was set in a New Jersey park in the middle of winter. So the kind folks in the wardrobe department bundled us all up in layered clothing and winter coats and sent us out into 90-plus degrees of summer heat. Talk about suffering for one's art.

It becomes even more difficult as one sits waiting for the grips and gaffers to set up the next shot. Terrifying introspection sets in like an encroaching fog. *Did I come here for this? Do I matter at all to this process? Is gracing the background the extent of my calling?* While I've run into one or two "career" background actors, most actors I know didn't come to Hollywood with background work as their highest aspiration. Some are even slightly embarrassed to admit they've done it, as if it is demeaning to their talent, a selling short of one's giftings.

So it's when those times of introspection hit that I try to smile, emotionally hitch up my trousers, and start looking for the deeper truths underlying the situation, those life lessons that help keep it all in perspective and that give me something to do as I stand in my wool overcoat under the unsympathetic sun, sweat trickling down my back.

Nobody wants to be a background actor. We live in a world that elevates the person in the spotlight. The player who is effective at drawing attention to himself is king, and the rest are too often relegated to the background as being of considerably lesser importance. And so, in our search for significance, it is to the point of distraction that we find ourselves striving to escape the obscurity of the background.

It's easy as modern-day believers to fall into this same mindset: spending a good amount of time, money, and energy trying to draw attention, trying to avoid falling into the background, trying to make certain that we – and our art, our churches, our ministries, our messages – are *seen*. It's not that marketing and promotions are necessarily bad. In fact, there's most certainly a place for it in this information age. But I wonder if the sheer volume of effort that we exert in trying to be noticed is a sign that we've missed the abundance of true life to which God calls us.

A city set on a hill cannot be hidden, Jesus said, in reference to us as believers. I wonder if we should focus more on being that city on the hill, rather than worrying about whether it can be seen or not. Because if that city is truly being what it is created to be, it doesn't have to worry about obscurity – according to Jesus, it *can't* be hidden. If the life of Christ is truly being exhibited in us, obscurity will be impossible. Rather than spending our time searching for the spotlight, the light will come from within.

When it comes down to it, our Christian movies, television, music, novels, and most everything else the Christian pop subculture generates to draw people's interest to Christianity are not really necessary to Christianity. Being a Christian is not primarily about finding a good means of drawing attention to the message of Christ, it is about being the message of Christ.

If I want to step out of the background, it will occur by vigorously being who God created me to be, by living out of the life that He puts inside of me. It is by that direction that each of us escapes the decline into obscurity.

DO NOT TRY TO PUSH YOUR WAY THROUGH
TO THE FRONT RANKS OF YOUR PROFESSION;
DO NOT RUN AFTER DISTINCTIONS AND AWARDS;
BUT DO YOUR UTMOST TO FIND AN ENTRY INTO
THE WORLD OF BEAUTY.

SYDNEY SMITH
Writer & Wit

28

Making Something Out Of Nothing

One of the things I hear pretty often from fellow creative artists as they wrestle with their aspirations – and especially those in the world of film – is that they don't have the equipment, finances, relationships, *(insert your own word here)* that they believe is needed to get started on their projects. Each of them can talk to me with great enthusiasm about that glorious project that he or she has in mind – and some of them are indeed glorious – but the final moments of the conversation tend to go something like this:

Artist:	...so that's what I want to do! What do you think?
Me:	That's a great idea!
Artist:	Thanks! I'm excited about it!
Me:	How far have you gotten on it?
Artist:	Um... Well, I haven't started yet...
Me:	What? You've got such a great idea, but you haven't done anything yet?
Artist:	Well, I... I don't have *(insert word again)*, so I'm waiting.
Me:	Waiting?
Artist:	Well, um... yes... like I said... ahem... *(trails off into uncomfortable silence)*.

It's a common stumbling block for artists: we can start thinking of everything we need to achieve the end result, and if just one of those things is missing, we end up never actually starting to create. Actually, most projects get their start by making something out of very little. In fact, there are ways even to make something out of nothing. Which is really like the first recorded act of creation by our Creator, a model by which we can shape all our artistic endeavors, which is summed up in the philosophical phrase *Ex nihilo*. For those of you who, like me, didn't retain anything from your Latin class, the phrase refers to the creation of something out of nothing.

In fact there are some pretty miraculous stories of folks, and One in particular, who, just for the fun of it, developed the habit of making a very real "plenty" out of a perceived "not enough."

Dive in there, get going, and you'll be amazed how often what you need to finish the project will present itself. I'm not going to say that is *always* the case, of course – our vision does indeed sometimes exceed our capacity – but it's the case more often than not.

Step up and step in, no matter what your artistic vision is. Even if you don't immediately have what you need to finish doesn't mean that you don't have what you need to start. So gather what little you've got and get out there...

YOU CAN'T CROSS THE SEA MERELY BY
STANDING AND STARING AT THE WATER.
RABINDRANATH TAGORE
Poet, Playwright, Painter & Musician

29
A Hard Truth

Dear Shun Lee,

In your observance of Christian artists in Hollywood and their speech with others, do you find them speaking the truths of the Bible – you know, the hard truths – or just speaking about "peace and love?" Jesus didn't always speak "pretty" things, but also what some would consider "down and dirty" truths. Thanks so much for all you do!

Sincerely,
Georgia

Dear Georgia,

Thank you for asking a good question. I suppose that the best answer to it is "yes." Here in the arts & entertainment industry, just like anywhere else, different Christians feel called to address different Biblical truths, including what you called the "hard truths." Some of them feel called to explore the meaning of peace and love; some of them feel called to speak about other truths. All of which are good, since real truth of any sort is worthy of consideration and communication, especially by artists.

Of course, no one truth exists in a vacuum; each requires

the other truths to give context to its meaning. The full frame of any virtue is comprised of the other virtues. Grace needs the truth of holiness to give it form and function. Holiness without grace is hard and suffocating. Mercy is best understood in the context of justice. Honor is best pursued in the exercise of discernment. Hope is made worthwhile by faith, and faith without works is dead. All the truths are intertwined.

In fact, any truth not understood in relationship to the other truths is amorphous at best, and at worst, dangerous. How often has lasting damage been done in the name of a solitary virtue – holiness, faith, love, grace, honor, hope, or any other noble concept – because it was adhered to without regard for the other virtues? Far too frequently. And so peace and love, without the benefit of the other truths, can (and often will) come across as a soft sell of an incomplete Gospel.

Peace and love, of course, are just as important and valuable as any other truths. Peace and love, when fully applied, are not always soft or pretty – although they are always beautiful. In fact, the practical application of peace and love in this world usually is downright messy. When we really consider the depth of what Jesus called us to in practicing real peace and love – here in Hollywood or anywhere else – we can begin to recognize how much these are hard truths as well. And as such, the truth about peace and love is worth the telling.

I've found that most creative artists have prophetic giftings – the longing and inclination to communicate the deep truths of God, even in environments that are not receptive to those truths. While those truths may be simple, they are never simplistic. I'm encouraged that so many artists who are Christians are endeavoring to speak up here in Hollywood, a place that too often resists those truths, and sometimes aggressively. With such artists here, and more on their way, there is truly hope for Hollywood and the arts and entertainment industry.

All my best,
Shun Lee

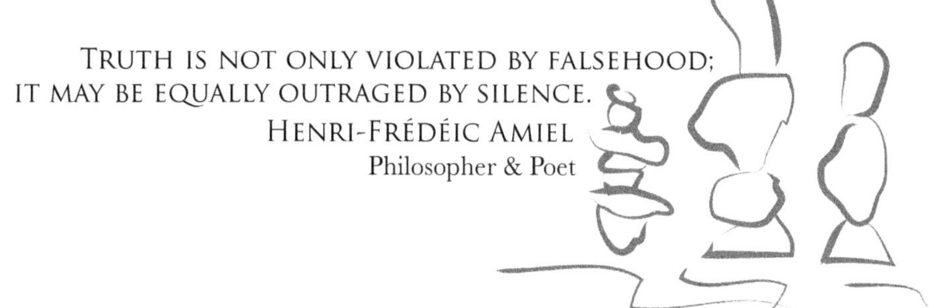

TRUTH IS NOT ONLY VIOLATED BY FALSEHOOD;
IT MAY BE EQUALLY OUTRAGED BY SILENCE.
HENRI-FRÉDÉIC AMIEL
Philosopher & Poet

30
Life In 4D

I had an amusing conversation the other day with a writer I've known for several years. This particular guy has a penchant for the comedic and the absurd, which always makes for interesting (although not always coherent) conversation between the two of us. I enjoy our discussions, especially since they tend to escape those useful, but often frustrating, constraints we know as "logic," and allow for a bit of imagination and suspended disbelief. Our chats often turn into an exercise in "believing six impossible things before breakfast," as Lewis Carroll once suggested.

This particular conversation turned to the recent trend in cinematography of filming and screening a movie three-dimensionally – or as you and I know it, in 3D. True to the absurdist nature of our previous exchanges, the question quickly came up (and I don't remember which one of us raised it) as to whether a certain well-known director would soon be shooting and screening films in *4D*. I mentioned the obvious fact that the first three dimensions are length, width, and depth, and then, purposefully ignoring time travel and the tesseract, I wondered out loud what that fourth dimension would look like in movie making.

"The four dimensions of film?" my friend wryly

responded. "That would be length, width, depth, and ego."

The world of the arts and entertainment is not the easiest field to navigate, in particular because of the overinflated egos that creative artists all too often develop. That sort of pride mucks up everything – creativity, relationships, business decisions – you name it. Usually, that sort of ego is a mask for an artist's own insecurities, but whatever the source may be, every creative person can fall prey to pride.

Unfortunately, that includes you and me. In fact, if you think you're exempt from the danger of pride, I'm afraid that you've already fallen into its clutches. And the problem with pride is that it distorts an artist's perspective about reality, and if there is anything that an artist must protect, it is his or her perspective. After all, art at its most basic definition is the communication of one's perspective. (Just what makes any particular work *good* art is a topic I'll save for another time.) All that to say that if you have a distorted perspective – even a distorted perspective of yourself, which is what pride takes great pleasure in creating – you will have a hard time being everything you were meant to be as an artist.

I hear many people pray, "Lord, make me humble," and perhaps rightly so, but they forget that the Bible instructs, "Humble *yourselves* in the sight of the Lord, and He will lift you up." Humility is my duty and yours; exalting is God's responsibility. Too often we spend our time doing the opposite: asking God to humble us while we spend all our time and energies lifting ourselves up, along with our own art and talents and abilities. What wonderful developments might occur if only we would just do our own job and trust God to do His?

So how do we find humility in a world full of egos? Allow me to offer some advice by way of a definition: *Humility is simply agreeing with what God says is true about you.* The good, the bad, and the ugly. Nothing more, nothing less.

In fact, some people swing to the opposite extreme of the overinflated ego by making themselves out to be less than they actually are. But this perspective of self is also in disagreement with what God says is true, and in the end, such people do just as much harm to themselves and others as their puffed-up counterparts do. That is only false humility, and I think you'll agree with me: Nothing stinks of true pride like false humility.

I think that my friend may have had it backwards. Perhaps *humility* is that elusive fourth dimension in film. For nothing is as beautiful and moving as ability and humility traveling together as one.

HUMILITY IS THE ONLY TRUE WISDOM
BY WHICH WE PREPARE OUR MINDS
FOR ALL THE POSSIBLE CHANGES OF LIFE.
GEORGE ARLISS
Actor, Writer & Filmmaker

31
Quoting Silence

Which is more powerful: the quarter-note tone or the quarter-note rest? I'd say that the answer is: each, in its place. I've heard it said that the real appreciation of jazz music is found in the notes you *don't* hear. In thinking about that, I've found it to be true. After all, so much can be said with silence.

I'm willing to wager that, like me, you have had the occasion to present to God one of those prayers that was, by your own reckoning, something big, momentous, and ripe for an answer from Him. *I don't understand* or *I have a need* or *Why didn't this work?* Or *When is it my turn?* I know that I've been there, those lean times when my knees have buckled and I've found myself seeking something, anything from God – a response, a retort, even a reprimand – only to be met with, of all things, silence.

But as with all things in the artistic life, we can and should find the purpose and meaning even in silence. In fact, the world would probably be a bit better off if we did so.

In our over-saturated society, we find ourselves overwhelmed by noise – visually, acoustically, and in every other way. We have become suspicious of silence, supposing – mistakenly, I would suggest – that if we do not see or hear something, then nothing is there. And because to many of us nothingness seems so undesirable – and I agree that it should – we attempt to fill up that space with just about everything we can.

I would hazard an opinion that some of our attempts to be "culturally relevant" are nothing more than adding to the cacophony, and that is an error on our part. Just because one has something to say doesn't mean that it should be said, a fact that too many artists overlook or conveniently forget.

Sometimes we are too quick to speak, too hasty with the pat answer, the prepared response. But sometimes God's response to us is silence. And we must not bring accusation against Him for that. Just because He is quiet doesn't mean that He isn't saying anything.

Yes, sometimes God's response to us is silence. And as artists created in His image, we must, in all our dealings with each other and the rest of the world, learn how to quote Him in this.

WELL-TIMED SILENCE HATH MORE ELOQUENCE THAN SPEECH.
MARTIN FRAQUHAR TUPPER
Author & Poet

32

Life's Own Aquifer

In case you're keeping tabs on my acting career, early next week I'm heading out with part of my creative team to Boiling Springs, Pennsylvania, to shoot a short film. I'm looking forward to being (or, if the cause should merit, not to being) in this hamlet, where we'll be shooting on one of the largest springs in the entire state.

Boiling Springs got its name from a naturally occurring artesian aquifer that emerges right in the center of town and which serves as the source of a waterway that winds through the Cumberland Valley. The aquifer draws water from a huge cavern 1,800 feet below the surface, the very heart of the earth. The tremendous pressure created in that underground cavern causes the water to bubble up to the surface, spilling out 22 million gallons of pure water every day, sustaining people, animals, plants, and more – and some of the best fly-fishing in the world. The water brings life wherever it goes.

It got me to thinking: what if someone were to steal in there in the dead of the night and hook up a source of pollution, maybe a sewer line, to the underground cavern? (My imagination too often tends toward super-villainy of the James Bond variety.) That polluted water would come gushing out, and everything it touched would be negatively affected by it. All the people, the animals, the life – all of that would get polluted as well. Everything would shrivel up and die because of the toxic water flowing from the source.

Proverbs 4:23 talks about how your heart is like that deep source of water: *Above all else, guard your heart, for it is the wellspring of life.* God is pretty serious when He says that. He's speaking of watching continuously over something extremely valuable. Think about it: we protect our cars and property from theft and damage, our bodies from sickness or injury, our creative ideas from undue influence, our business and financial interests from failure, even our borders from terrorist attacks. And here God says, "That's all well and good, but your heart is even more important, and *you're* responsible for it, *you're* the one who needs to take extra security measures."

You have to guard your heart above anything else you have, because it affects everything you do. It's your life's own aquifer. It's the source, the wellspring of everything you do and say and are. Jesus even went so far to say, "For the mouth speaks out of that which fills the heart. The good man brings out of his good treasure what is good; and the evil man brings out of his evil treasure what is evil." *(Matt.12:34b-35)* What is in your heart, the center of who you are, ultimately ends up determining the actions you take, the words you say, the emotions you have, the art you create – the kind of life you're going to live.

When it comes down to it, the primary cause of all the brokenness we see around us in this world isn't economics, politics, social pressures, or other external things. The fact is that more individual loss and societal ruin has been caused by people failing to protect their hearts from pollution – anger, pride, lust, shame, offenses, fear, unforgiveness, and more –

than all those other external areas combined.

It's like the Enemy of your soul, a super-villain in his own right, found a way to get that pollution in there. And the problem is that as time goes on, your heart begins to leak, spilling pollution into all the things you say and do, and out over yourself and everyone around you. So everybody just ends up getting slimed, becoming angrier, less tolerant, more impatient. And that just spreads the pollution even further.

So what if you had to drink from the river of *your* heart? What if somebody else did, perhaps even somebody you love? Would it be like drinking from a polluted stream and making everyone around you do the same?

Take a look at your heart, and I'll take a look at mine. It requires a lot of honesty and courage, but you can tell plenty about yourself by what comes spilling out. If what is flowing out is polluted – in your art, your business dealings, your relationships – it's time for a clean-up. When the source is clean, what flows from it is clean too, and that frees you to begin bringing life to yourself and everything around you.

THERE ARE MOMENTS IN LIFE,
WHEN THE HEART IS SO FULL OF EMOTION
THAT IF BY CHANCE IT BE SHAKEN
OR INTO ITS DEPTHS LIKE A PEBBLE
DROPS SOME CARELESS WORD, IT OVERFLOWS,
AND ITS SECRET, SPILT ON THE GROUND LIKE WATER,
CAN NEVER BE GATHERED TOGETHER.

HENRY WADSWORTH LONGFELLOW
Poet

33

For Those Who Mourn

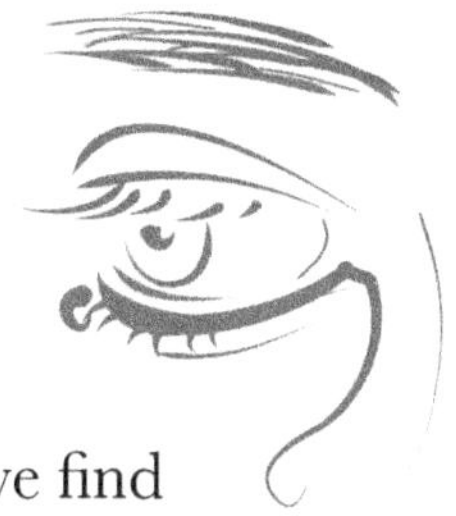

I hope you will permit me to be transparent with you and perhaps ramble a bit here. It is appropriate to allow the inner workings of our lives to seep into the words we write, the images we capture, the sounds we create. If we are not forthcoming in our art, where else will we find relief?

My grandmother passed away unexpectedly Sunday evening. I have to admit, the last couple of days have been filled with sorrow for me. I loved my grandmother. She and I have been close, and she has been a warm presence in my life as long as I can remember. So the grief when I received the news late that night was deep and immediate.

I'm going to miss her strength and care. I'm going to miss the prayers she continuously offered up for me and my brothers and sisters. I'm going to miss the crisp two-dollar bills she would save up and send me each Valentine's Day and Easter. I'm going to miss her secret recipe of potato salad and her pot roast. I'm going to miss *her*.

We are uncomfortable with grief in our culture, and we will do most anything we can to inoculate ourselves against it.

But in our haste, we forget that grief does not always damage. Sometimes it heals. And we do a disservice to ourselves and to those around us when our response to grief is to try to extricate from it at the first opportunity.

It is not appropriate nor is it biblical to immediately cheer up those who are immersed in grief. *Mourn with those who mourn.* Our job is not to pull them out of grief, but to join them there. To bear the burden of grief with them. This was the ministry of Jesus Christ, and so must it be for us.

I would suggest that this is especially true of us who are artists.

In our culture, we as believers are too often not taken seriously because we have yet to truly take the grief of the world seriously. We are so busy trying to extricate or distract them from it that we forget that the grief is *real*, *substantial*, and most of all, *appropriate*. Grief is the reminder that we have fallen, we are broken, and we are in desperate need of repair. We are haunted by our memories of Eden. We have lost something, and even with the redemptive life of Christ, grief is the reminder at the deepest part of who we are that things are not as they were meant to be.

That doesn't mean that we should be defined by our sorrows or that the promises of God aren't true. In His time, He will indeed turn our mourning into dancing; He most certainly will wipe away every tear. But we don't want to rush grief. To attempt to simply remove ourselves or others from grief is to trivialize the role that it has in this life. It trivializes who we are as people.

In its own way, grief is a grace, because it illuminates. And as I sit beneath its pounding light, let me finish with this: we are artists, and as artists, ours is the job of reminding people of what is truly important in this world and the world to come, and how we can, somehow, experience the latter in the former.

Look well, my fellow artists, and with care, for there are some things in this world that do not matter.

THERE IS AN ALCHEMY IN SORROW.
IT CAN BE TRANSMUTED INTO WISDOM,
WHICH, IF IT DOES NOT BRING JOY,
CAN YET BRING HAPPINESS.
PEARL S. BUCK
Novelist

34

Letter To a Crazy Friend: Strange Work

My Dear Crazy Friend,

Thanks for your recent note of encouragement! It was good to hear from you, and your encouraging words couldn't have come at a better time.

I noticed in your letter that perhaps you could use a little encouragement yourself. I know both by observation and reputation that you've been working hard at your craft and career and that you bring a lot of talent and ideas to the table. But as you hinted in your letter, in spite of all your prominent abilities, you feel as if you've encountered a wall that stands in the way of moving forward in your career. And it's hard not to notice all the other people who seem to get to bypass that wall altogether, leaving you feeling frustrated and maybe just a little bit… well, jealous.

I've stood before that wall too, with nothing better to do than count the bricks that stand between me and achievement. In fact, every artist I've known who is worth his or her salt has stood there too, even those ones who currently seem to be moving forward with ease while you stand there and wait.

It's a funny thing about being an artist. It requires a tremendous amount of faith to get up every day and try to move forward, and we'd like to believe that God sees that faith and rewards it with breakthrough. And I'm here to tell you that He actually does, in spite of the fact that you've now hit this obstacle that has you at a standstill. It's just that His breakthrough may not look anything like what you expected.

When it comes down to it, God doesn't make a lot of sense to us sometimes – in fact, sometimes He comes across as just plain odd. We really shouldn't be surprised by His quirky ways, however, since He pretty much warned us that He was going to work that way in our lives. I was reading a Bible passage this morning that couldn't be any more clear about that fact:

> *The LORD will rise up as he did at Mount Perazim, he will rouse himself as in the Valley of Gibeon – to do his work, his strange work, and perform his task, his alien task. (Isaiah 28:21)*

It appears that God, who is good, has plans that just seems strange to us. Oddly enough, the Hebrew name of the mountain mentioned in that verse is instructive as well – *Perazim* means "breakthrough". Which is to say that the breakthrough He has for you more than likely will come about by His strange work too.

John the Baptist, one of the great heroes of the faith, had to struggle with God's strange ways of doing business too. After years of proclaiming that Jesus was the promised Messiah who would deliver God's people, John unjustly ended up sitting, of all places, in prison. Disappointed and wondering whether he had been wrong about Jesus in the first place, John sent a few messengers to find out whether he had made a big mistake. Jesus told the messengers to go back to John and report that all the prophecies that had foretold the signs of the Messiah's coming were indeed happening – miraculous wonders were occurring and the good news of God's Kingdom was being given freely to everyone. And then Jesus said something that cut to the quick of John's real question of disappointment:

> *Blessed is he who does not take offense at Me. (Luke 7:23)*

You see, God has His strange ways of doing things, and sometimes they can seem painful, unintelligible, and even downright obstructive to the very thing He has called you to do. Anyone who implies to you that you will always understand what God is up to has not yet fully lived life. In the end, however, God promises blessings for those who can embrace His strange ways without being offended by Him.

So take heart, my dear Crazy Friend: God sees the big picture of His Kingdom and the role He created you to play in it, and He is actively taking steps to ensure that you *do* play that role. As in all the good things He does, it just may take some strange work to get there. God's ways may be strange, but they sure are extraordinary.

Your Crazy Friend,
Shun Lee

IF YOU CAN FIND A PATH WITH NO OBSTACLES,
IT PROBABLY DOESN'T LEAD ANYWHERE.
FRANK HOWARD CLARK
Screenwriter

35

Contentment

I've been going through one of my old journals, reminiscing and reflecting on thoughts gone by. The other day, I ran across an old entry I wrote about three years ago:

> *I'm sitting here in this diner in North Hollywood, and I am surprised by a sense of peace. There is a football game on the television behind the bar. I've been slowly soaking in the ideas that drip from a book of conversations with Bono. The coffee isn't half bad, and outside, the September sun is smiling. The diner is partially full, and so are the diners, and so there is a warmth that saturates the place; this is no hurried pace. There is a beautiful girl who has brought me my food, and she stops by to refill my coffee – but her smile tells me this is a pretext. My ambitions melt away, leaving only contentment, and for a moment, I am touched with the briefest realization: with all this, God is pleased.*

Contentment. I'm struck by how rare a commodity it is here in Hollywood, where ambition and hunger and the pursuit of more are held in such high regard.

It's not that contentment and desire can't reside in the same heart. They most certainly can; they are not mutually exclusive. But we must be sure to not displace desire with dissatisfaction.

The condition of the human heart is such that we each search for contentment – at least until something better comes along. We were created for contentment in our relationship with God and with the broad abundance He created for His pleasure and for our resource. Our attentions can be so consumed by the things and positions and opportunities that we do not yet have that we forget to bask in the wonderful wealth, that abundant beauty and grace, that God doles out like a joyful spendthrift.

The thing about contentment is that, by its very nature, it is not something we strive to achieve; it is, rather, something we either accept or reject. So ask yourself this week, and I will too: Could it be that the *more* we're desperately searching for already lies around us for the accepting?

I AM CONTENT; THAT IS A BLESSING GREATER THAN RICHES; AND HE TO WHOM THAT IS GIVEN NEED ASK NO MORE.

HENRY FIELDING
Novelist & Playwright

36

Outside A Stained Glass Window

In late 2002, I went on a nine-day trip with my father to Hong Kong, which is where he grew up. I already was several years into a successful professional career, so it required taking some time off from a busy schedule. But my dad and I saw this as an opportunity to do some good ol' Father & Son bonding, so I was glad to go.

We had a great time on the trip. We traveled all over that expansive city by planes, trains, and automobiles, checking out my dad's old stomping grounds and meeting distant relatives for the first time. And I kept an eye out for any and all McDonald's, since, when God created me, He apparently decided to flex his sense of irony. ("Hey, watch this: let's make him be Chinese *and* hate Chinese food. Come on, it'll be *funny*!")

There's something just a tad precarious about a God who is omnipotent and has a sense of humor.

One stop on our tour that stood out to me was St. John's Cathedral, the oldest Anglican church building in the Far East, having opened its doors in 1849. When we arrived, a memorial service for a well-known Hong Kong dignitary was coming to a close, and outside there were dozens of flower arrangements sent by many of the city's elite. (I remember, in particular, a large bouquet that film star Jackie Chan had offered.) My dad and I sat down in the shade to watch the people as they offered condolences to one another before leaving.

Once the church building had cleared out, we walked inside to take a look. What impressed me the most was the massive stained-glass window set in the east wall of the chancel. It was a beautiful piece of art, a towering collection of vivid color depicting Jesus Christ on the Mount of Crucifixion, as Mary, His mother, and Mary Magdalene stood nearby weeping. This wonderful stained glass artwork captured a moment and told a story. The light that poured through all these pieces of glass arranged together illuminated the entire sanctuary and everyone in it.

After my dad and I left the building, however, we got a different view of this same piece of stained glass art. The church's east wall runs right next to the street, and as we made our way down the sidewalk, I looked up at the window. From outside the church, the window was not a beautiful story or piece of artwork; it was only a tangled mess of soldered lead and rough, mismatched glass fragments. From that outside perspective, I couldn't tell what the glasswork was trying to say at all, and I certainly couldn't see Jesus in it.

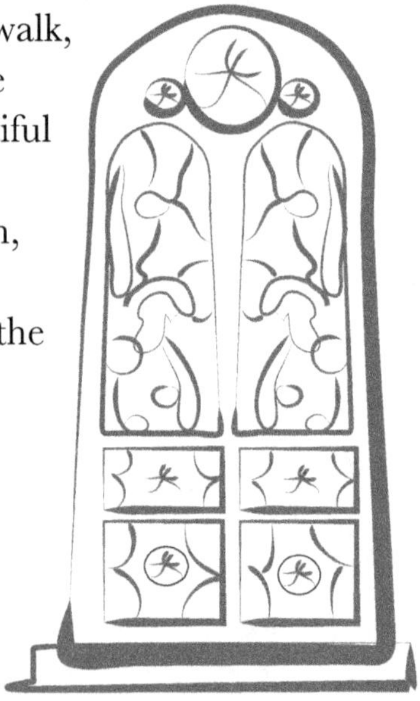

Understanding perspective is key to being a creative artist. Not only should the artist be able to effectively present his own perspective through his medium, but he must also take into consideration the perspective of his viewers. Too often, creative artists forget this, and especially in niche genres like faith-based art: it illuminates and makes sense to people on the inside of the church, but not to anyone on the outside. That's okay, I guess, if the artwork is intended *solely* for the people on the inside, but it is a failure if it is also intended for the people who are outside, because it is nothing but a tangled mess to them. The artist has not communicated to the outsiders.

But it isn't just in faith-based art that this occurs. It's in any type of art that communicates to an audience without taking into consideration their perspective, without providing them with a context by which they are able to understand. And the problem is that, given this breakdown in communication, too many artists would rather blame the audience members for being outsiders than make the effort to provide them with that context which would allow them to understand. This is artistic elitism.

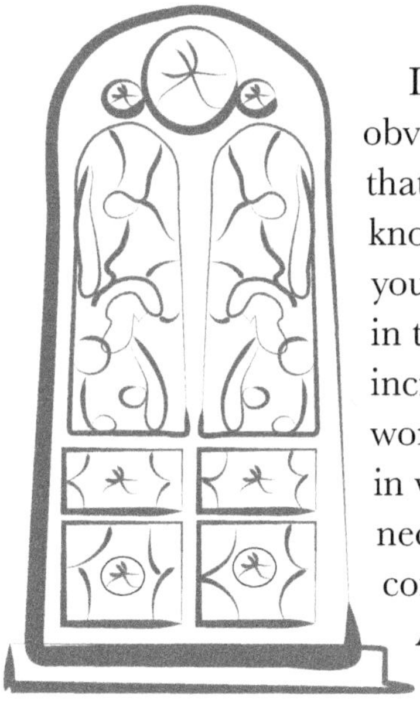

It's not that your art has to be blatant or obvious – in fact, you usually want to avoid that. There's something important about knowing how to conceal truth within your creation so that the viewer engages in the process of searching for it. But the increasing diversity and pluralism of our world has created a fragmented culture in which the people around you do not necessarily share the same background, convictions and values that you do. As a result, to assume that they will understand what you are trying to convey from your insider's view will likely lead only to failed communication.

As you create this week in your own artistic endeavors, take some time to get a little perspective – other than just your own. Ask yourself who your intended viewers are and whether you actually are communicating in a way they can understand. If you aren't, take a step back from your artwork for a moment and reassess how to broaden its scope so that they too are on the inside, so that they too can be illuminated.

THE SINGLE BIGGEST PROBLEM IN COMMUNICATION
IS THE ILLUSION THAT IT HAS TAKEN PLACE.

GEORGE BERNARD SHAW

Playwright, Literary Critic & Essayist

37

THE LAST MINUTE

The other day, I sent off a film proposal and script treatment to a potential financier. I had worked hard on the proposal and treatment, spending several weeks putting them together, especially because this financier had shown a great degree of interest in the project in the several conversations we'd had about it. I attached the documents to the email and hit the *Send* button. Suddenly, the process was out of my hands, and I found myself sitting in my office… waiting.

Okay, full confession: I hate waiting. It grates against my can-do, get-things-accomplished, Type-A personality, mostly because 1) it feels like nothing is happening, and 2) there's not a thing I can do about it. I have no control. Oh, don't get me wrong – I've got plenty of other things to do, some good ideas and projects that I'm excited about getting off the ground. But in the back of my mind, there's this gnawing impatience to have an answer for *that* project. I want *that* one to fly now, and instead I find myself waiting for clearance from air traffic control. So I sit on the runway and wait, with plenty of time to stew over any number of thoughts – primarily, how much I hate waiting.

Why is it that God makes us wait? Yeah, sure, I know that He is sovereign and understands the big picture much better than I do, but *why* does He make us wait? In His omnipotent sovereignty, couldn't He just rearrange all the elements so that I *don't* have to wait? I mean, come on! What's the big hold-up here? I'm willing to bet that you have a few things you find yourself waiting for too – artistically, financially, relationally, or otherwise. Maybe all of the above.

It's enough to make God look capricious, almost mean. But perhaps there's a reason for all this waiting beyond what I can see. Perhaps there is something about the process that is just as important as the end result – or even more so.

If you take a look in the Bible, just about every person who had a waiting period and embraced it went on to great success. Conversely, every person in the Bible who either didn't have a waiting period or didn't embrace the waiting period that God gave him or her – eventually failed. Which, of course, makes sense: the perseverance that the waiting produces in us (if we let it) is what gives us the character that ultimately is necessary for true success. Just because I don't like it doesn't make it any less true: the waiting makes me stronger.

But not only does God make us wait, He often makes us wait until the last minute. In fact, in my experience, not only does He make me wait until the last minute, He often makes me wait until after what I think is the last minute. God makes us wait until after the last minute because He wants to make sure our hope is in Him, and not in our ability to hold out for the last minute. God wants our trust to be in *Him*, and not in our own ability to trust. The waiting purges us of our misplaced reliance on our own abilities, even our abilities to trust and persevere.

If God has foisted some waiting on you, see how quickly things change when you embrace it. After all, there's a whole lot happening while you wait.

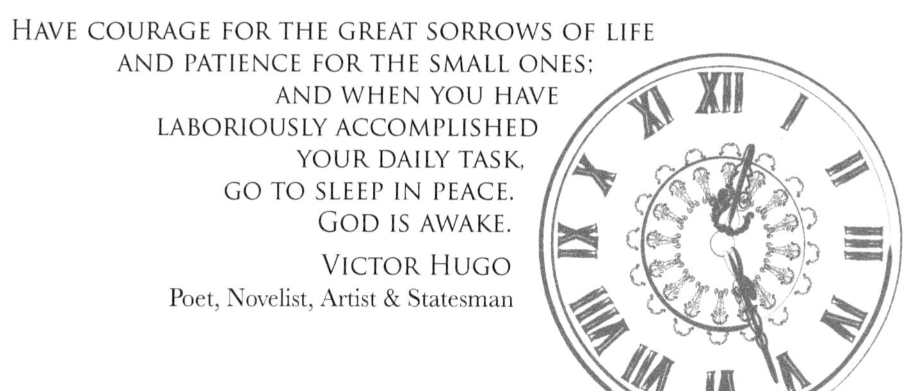

HAVE COURAGE FOR THE GREAT SORROWS OF LIFE
AND PATIENCE FOR THE SMALL ONES;
AND WHEN YOU HAVE
LABORIOUSLY ACCOMPLISHED
YOUR DAILY TASK,
GO TO SLEEP IN PEACE.
GOD IS AWAKE.

VICTOR HUGO
Poet, Novelist, Artist & Statesman

38

Know What You Write

There is an old axiom for writers that I think is equally appropriate for all art forms: *Write what you know.* Okay, okay, this isn't a hard-and-fast rule; I highly doubt that J.R.R. Tolkien had spent any appreciable time with elves and hobbits or that George Lucas had set foot on the *Millennium Falcon* when they first set pens to paper. Taking the "*write what you know*" maxim too far – that is, exclusively creating based on what you've personally experienced – would not only rule out any science fiction, fantasy, and anything featuring Jack Bauer, it also would effectively reduce all creativity to autobiography.

But like most axioms, "*write what you know*" is a fair generalization that can lead to good results. It comes, like many other rules of creativity, from sound principles of making sure you know your subject, that you've done your research, and that you've checked your terminology and facts. It's not that you can't write or act or direct without that full understanding of your subject – you can – but it is that understanding that your audience will be looking for in your writing or acting or directing. Nothing is worse than taking in that piece of work by which the artist reveals that he has no idea what he's talking about.

Good writing – and good art of any sort – invites its audience to relate to and live through someone else's experience. So it does little good for the audience member to enter into the work and discover that no experience exists there, or worse yet, that the experience is not true or even related to life – to the way this world is and to people, their emotions, and their motivations.

The "*write what you know*" adage serves as a reminder to us as artists to actually *know* something, to gain some experience of life, before we sit down to create. We must be careful to not get so wrapped up in creating our art that we forget that there is a world out there, ripe for participation, that God created for us to experience and then interpret through our art. We mustn't forget this, especially in light of some of our tendencies toward near-obsessive focus on our artwork. We can be so eager to capture life in our art that we forget to experience life.

That can't be what God intended for us when He made us artists.

We were meant to engage with the world around us – to stretch and yawn, set down the pen, and go out and live a little. It's good for us artistically and spiritually. Talk with people and find out what makes them unique. Wander through the mall, in the fields, down the canyons. Play, and when you have done that, play some more. Cultivate your curiosity. Watch how people conduct themselves at work and

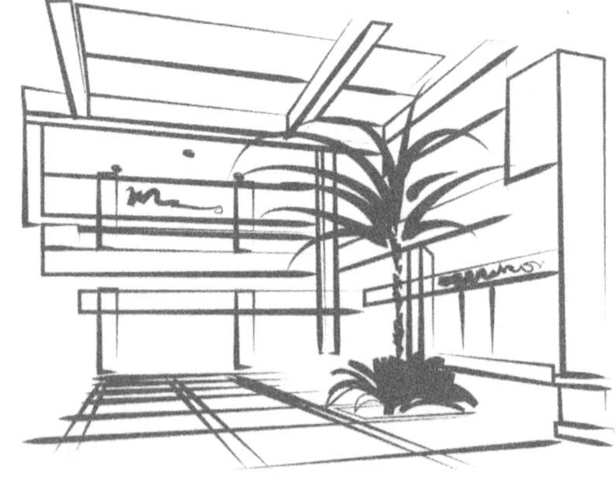

in recreation. Go observe how people *really* behave in church and in prayer – as they are, not as you think they should be. In the process of all this, gather as much experience as you can – it is your currency as an artist. From this world, the real one, we draw our inspiration for creating something that speaks of a world beyond it.

Then sit back down and recreate what you saw, reflect it in your work. If you've done it right and you've done it enough, your audience will see that you actually do have an idea of what you're talking about.

HOW VAIN IT IS TO SIT DOWN TO WRITE
WHEN YOU HAVE NOT STOOD UP TO LIVE.
HENRY DAVID THOREAU
Author, Philosopher & Poet

39

Positive/Negative

I'm writing this article on the seventh anniversary of the day I first arrived in Los Angeles to begin my Hollywood adventure as a professional actor and writer. I've heard it said that you should always take time to celebrate the small victories, and in my book, any time you're able to say you've done something for seven years, that's a pretty good victory.

It's been a great journey, filled with all the highs and lows and uncertainties found in any good adventure. The best part, aside from being able to do something that I absolutely love doing and getting paid for it, is the number of wonderfully interesting people I've met along the way. Yes, this adventure has been filled with artists, entrepreneurs, supporters, and fans, many of whom I'm honored to now call my friends.

I've lived just long enough to know that true friends – the sort who not only will prop you up on the lean days, but who will also avoid running up the tab on your abundant ones – are exceedingly rare. I've been blessed to have them in my corner, and I'm sure you can think of a few in your own. As artists, we need people like that around us. Artistry, which so often occurs in solitude, should never be solitary.

Of course, not everyone you'll run across in your artistic journey has the personality or inclination to be that sort of support for you.

Take, by way of example, the gentleman from my hometown who, during my first year in Los Angeles, always managed to slip into his every communication with me some version of the question, "When are you giving up and coming home?" as if it was a foregone conclusion. Or the woman here in Los Angeles who always wanted to partner with me in brainstorming some creative ideas, only to shoot down each and every one I offered with a litany of reasons why it wouldn't work.

Not everybody will be on your side, I'm afraid. You occasionally will meet the person – perhaps even a fellow artist! – who will go to great lengths, consciously or not, to make you feel smaller because it provides her with the silly illusion that she has somehow grown bigger.

Be forewarned: you will meet people who are predisposed to relate to others in this way. Accepting that fact ahead of time makes it easier to respond when you inevitably cross paths with one. You'll be able to face his or her negativity with a curious look and a "*Huh. You're one of them,*" before you continue on your way without giving it another thought. You'll be able to run across them without succumbing to the urge to run over them.

I should add, of course: take care not to be one of those people yourself.

Some people expend all their creative strength in coming up with reasons why certain things can't be done. Avoid such people. Instead, surround yourself with those who spend their creative strength in the realm of faith and possibilities.

That's not to say that you should never listen when someone offers a critique. After all, your true friends are there to keep you grounded in reality, not just to inflate your ego. But learn to discern who those true friends are. The people with whom you want to surround yourself are those whose critiques are intended to help you grow into more of who you were created to be, not just to point out that you are less.

Cultivate those relationships. Cultivate that kind of community, that kind of creative environment. If you find yourself surrounded by the naysayers, find a polite but firm way to disentangle yourself. It's worth the effort. And when *your* artistic anniversary rolls around, like me, you'll be able to say you did it all with help from a few of your friends.

KEEP AWAY FROM THOSE WHO TRY TO BELITTLE YOUR AMBITIONS. SMALL PEOPLE ALWAYS DO THAT, BUT THE REALLY GREAT MAKE YOU BELIEVE THAT YOU TOO CAN BECOME GREAT.

MARK TWAIN
Author & Humorist

40

Breaking The Rules

Those of you who know me personally or who have spent any amount of time reading my column will know that I used to be an attorney, a profession with which I'm glad to now be unencumbered. While the practice of law is a high and noble calling for certain people, during *my* season as a corporate and trial attorney, I found that in spite of my expertise, I was getting tired of seeing the worst sides of people each and every day – the egos, the greed, the petty arguments over contractual minutiae.

So I made the only logical choice and moved to the entertainment industry.

One of the few humorous aspects of the legal profession is that every so often one runs across some archaic and often arcane rules that still pepper the law books. These are laws that, at one point or another, probably made sense to some legislative body, but it's hard to see how. Don't believe me? Here are a few examples of state and municipal laws that are still on the books in California today:

- *It is a misdemeanor to shoot any kind of game from a moving vehicle, unless the target is a whale.* (California)
- *Peacocks have the right of way to cross any street, including driveways.* (Arcadia)

- *You are not allowed to wear cowboy boots unless you already own two cows.* (Blythe)
- *A man can't go outside while wearing a jacket and pants that don't match.* (Carmel)
- *Detonating a nuclear device within the city limits results in a $500 fine.* (Chico)
- *A person may not drive more than 2,000 sheep down Hollywood Boulevard at one time.* (Hollywood)
- *You may not bathe two babies in the same tub at the same time.* (Los Angeles)
- *It is illegal to carry a fish into a bar.* (Portola)
- *A motor vehicle may not be driven on city streets unless a man with a lantern walks ahead of it.* (Redlands)
- *It's illegal to wipe one's car with used underwear.* (San Francisco)
- *Kites may not be flown more than 10 feet above the ground.* (Walnut)

You may have broken one or more of these laws yourself. If so, you know who you are. The problem with such violations, however, is that you don't even get the pleasure of that spine-tingling thrill of rebelliousness that comes with intentionally breaking the rules, because I'm willing to bet you didn't even know they were rules in the first place.

It's that way with your artistic endeavors too. Every art form has certain rules that are inherent to it, whether that form is writing, acting, filmmaking, painting, or something else. With that said, there is a place to break those rules sometimes. In fact, some creative artists have become truly great *because* they broke the rules – think of Picasso's Cubist paintings, Hitchcock's technical breakthroughs in filmmaking, or e.e. cumming's poetry that played fast and loose with punctuation and capitalization.

If you want to stand out as such an artist, one who has become renowned because you're able to bend and break the rules of your art form, you must first know and study what those rules actually are. An artist who fails to do so isn't really breaking the rules; he's just putting his ignorance on display. So before you go trying to break the rules, learn what they are and how to keep them.

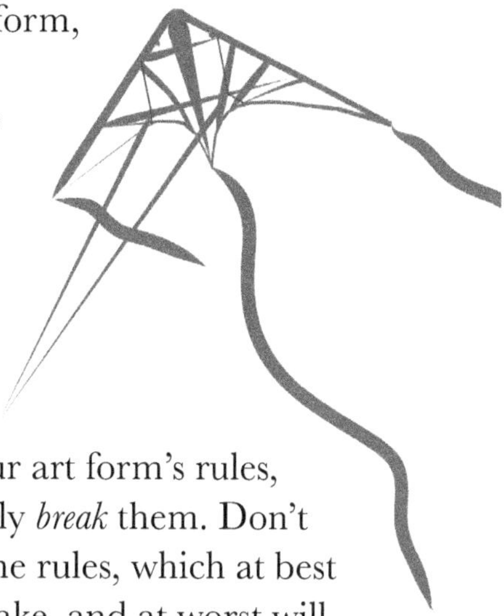

Then, if you're going to break your art form's rules, for goodness' sakes, don't skimp. Really *break* them. Don't just wander around on the edges of the rules, which at best will only look like you've made a mistake, and at worst will look like you have no idea what you're doing.

Third, if you do decide to break the rules, be prepared to take some flack. There are some people who will be quite vocal about the fact that you broke the rules. Unfortunately, many of them will be artists in your own field – your *peers* – many of whom have been following those artistic rules for a long time. Perhaps ever since they broke the rules that preceded *them* years and years ago. And the worst part of it all will be that you will actually have to listen respectfully to what they have to say, because they might actually have some constructive feedback. Please notice, however, that I didn't say you have to agree with them. Once you have milked every ounce of insight from their critiques, you may find that the best thing is to go on breaking those artistic rules.

Take a look at your own artistic endeavors. Have you truly learned the rules of your art form? If not, take the time to understand them and why they are considered rules – this can only be learned in the practice of them. But when you have them down, I encourage you to start systematically taking risks by finding ways to bend and break those rules with a sense of consistency and in the pursuit of good craft.

Of course, you may also have to help people understand what you're doing, so be ready to give a good explanation for your decisions. At first, it will sound as sensible as explaining why you're marching 2,001 sheep down Hollywood Boulevard or carrying a fish into a bar, but you may find that some of those rules are there just to be broken.

I ALWAYS SAY THAT IT IS ABOUT BREAKING THE RULES.
BUT THE SECRET OF BREAKING RULES IN A WAY THAT WORKS IS UNDERSTANDING WHAT THE RULES ARE IN THE FIRST PLACE.
RICK WAKEMAN
Musician, Songwriter, Author & Actor

41

Facing the Blank Page

Facing the blank page. It's that terrifying time in which you sit down to create, and the bare paper lies there before you, staring back, daring you to make that first stroke. The fear, of course, is that the first stroke will not only fail to be a masterful one, but that it just might ruin the page altogether. Different types of artists struggle with "blank page syndrome," but all artists have their own version of it. Writers, painters, and composers encounter it quite literally, but even if you're not one of those, I'm willing to bet that you also have had to deal with it in your own way.

If you find yourself in that place of creativity, here are a few tips for tackling the blank page:

1. Make it easier for yourself by remembering that you aren't the only one who has had to sit there, waiting for inspiration. The mere fact that everybody has to deal with this struggle is encouraging in its own way. They made it past the blank page, and so will you. So quit being so hard on yourself.

2. Remember that the blank page is not an obstacle; it's a playground. When you start viewing that empty space as an opportunity to play and experiment, rather than as your antagonist, you free yourself up to try new things, to experiment, to discover, and even to fail without fear. The

blank page becomes a world of possibilities.

3. Try starting with an outline or a game plan before you actually sit down to start creating. This will give you a general road map to follow. Preplanning pays off in the manner of that old truism: *An ounce of prevention is worth a pound of cure.* But don't get so locked into your road map that you don't make room for creative surprises.

4. Get some exercise in before you start creating. It's a very different approach than what your high school writing teacher tried to get you to do – to sit still and just write. Physical exercise gets the blood flowing, and that's been shown to increase mental function and creativity. Take a walk or hit the gym or even stretch for a few minutes.

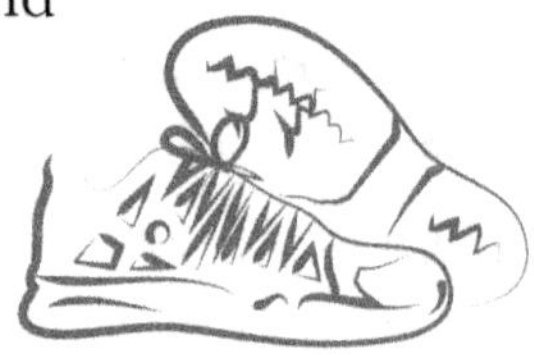

5. Just do something. Sometimes you have to simply dive in and create, knowing that the creative process is (and really should be) messy, which means that it doesn't have to be perfect. Of course, that means you can't start with an attitude of self-editing or self-criticism. Just create, and later you can go back and clean up, edit, or even erase at your leisure.

I'm sure you can think of a few other ideas for approaching the blank canvas of creativity – whether you are a writer, a composer, an actor, or any other type of artist. If so, send your ideas my way.

I LOVE THE BLANK PAGE...
I DON'T KNOW WHY WRITERS COMPLAIN ABOUT IT.
I FIND IT HARD TO STARE AT A PAGE THAT HAS WORDS ON IT.
THE BLANK PAGE IS A BIG OPEN INVITATION.

ED SOLOMON
Screenwriter, Film Producer & Director

42

Escaping a Terminal Life

I've been thinking a lot lately about fear and courage. What is this stuff called Courage that we all aspire to, that so inspires us, but in the end, even for the best of us, can be so tantalizingly elusive? We lionize those who have the nerve to summon it up and make it stick, and rightly so. So it has me wondering: Where do we find Courage; where does it reside? What is the shape of Courage, and what does it look like?

Many of you may have seen the Steven Spielberg film, *The Terminal.* For those of you who haven't seen it yet, it's about a man who, because of political strife that essentially dissolves the government in his home country, gets stranded in John F. Kennedy International Airport for an entire year. Armed with a passport from nowhere, the U.S. government will not allow him to enter the country, and yet, he has no country to which he can return. And so he becomes the accidental tourist, living a life in limbo in the airport terminal from which he has no place to go.

What you may not know is that this story is based upon the life of a real person, an Iranian by the name of Alfred Merhan. Merhan lived on a bench in Terminal 1 of Paris's Charles de Gaulle Airport from 1988 until he was hospitalized in 2006. That's 18 years. When he first arrived at the airport, he basically became stuck in a political holding pattern:

because of previous militant activities, his home country wouldn't have him back; but no other country would grant him asylum. So he stayed in Terminal 1, getting comfortable in his new surroundings, eating the available food, living in a shrunken world that had all the focused busyness of real life, but very little of the freedom.

In 1999, the French authorities decided that Merhan had suffered enough. They granted him the one thing that would release him from that great bustling microcosm of an airport by giving him refugee status. But the very next day, Merhan was found still sitting on his bench in Terminal 1.

Months later, representatives from Spielberg's production company came to that bench in Terminal 1. They paid Merhan $300,000 for the rights to his life story (which they significantly altered to create *The Terminal*, by the way). Merhan was grateful. He put the money in his pocket and continued to sit on his bench.

A man with wealth fit for a king in his pocket and airplanes leaving every few minutes all around him, and yet he sat there. Ironic, isn't it? The odd thing is that Merhan dreamed of escaping to the outside world. In an interview with a Reuters reporter, he confided, "I don't want to stay forever, but I'm happy with it as a short-term solution. I don't feel like I'm in prison. I'm not bored." And yet, for 18 years he never ventured more than 100 yards outside of the airport.

My purpose for bringing this up isn't to disparage Merhan. To be honest, I don't know what motivated him. But I do know what motivates me to get stuck in my own private airports.

One of the statements of bumper-sticker theology that I disagree with the most is this one: *The safest place to be is in the center of God's will.* Having been in Hollywood for a while now, I don't buy that for a second. For one thing, if we believe that, we run the risk of confusing safety with God's will. After all, if God's will means safety, then anytime we're safe, it must mean we're in God's will. That's simple logic! It's a case of x equals y, so y must equal x, right?

Wrong. Quite frankly, I can be safe in my own private airport, getting used to my surroundings, eating the available food, and experiencing all the focused busyness, and still not be walking in the life for which God created me, artistically or otherwise. Instead of letting perfect love drive out fear, I end up putting myself in positions where it's difficult to encounter fear in the first place.

On the other hand, some of the scariest places in the world are where God's presence is.

The other problem with that bumper-sticker theology is that it gets us longing for the wrong thing. If we're only searching for safety, we will be missing out not only on the Adventures that God has called each of us to, but also on the very character of God Himself. Because when it comes down to it, while God can grant us safety at times, He is not very safe. He is very, very dangerous.

Of course, that dangerousness is encapsulated – though not tempered – by His goodness. Good and dangerous. The temptation is to want all of His goodness, and none of His danger. But to worship part of His character and deny another part is only to create a god in the image of my choosing. I dare not. I dare not worship the Lamb of God and avoid the Lion of Judah. Rather, I must learn to revel in His dangerousness as much as I do His goodness. And in so doing, recognize that He often calls us to dangerous things.

So many times, the thing that keeps us from stepping out into the danger of the Adventures to which we know that God is calling us is, simply put, fear. I'm slowly finding, though, that if I intentionally walk forward, I discover that fear is almost always a great, big, ugly… puff of air. There is an incomparable thrill to walking in and through it like a hazy mist, finding that God was there all along in the middle of it all, and discovering what is on the other side. The danger of the situation may be tangible, but the fear becomes much less so.

What is the shape of Courage, and where does it reside? This is an important lesson for us artists to learn: Courage is discovered only in the midst of fear – courage without fear is not courage, it is bravado – and so we must each intentionally enter in and do that thing of which we are afraid. It is there, with a spiritual wealth fit for a king in our pockets, that we will keep our life stories from becoming terminal ones.

TWENTY YEARS FROM NOW YOU WILL BE
MORE DISAPPOINTED BY THE THINGS
THAT YOU DIDN'T DO THAN BY THE ONES YOU DID DO.
SO THROW OFF THE BOWLINES.
SAIL AWAY FROM THE SAFE HARBOR.
CATCH THE TRADE WINDS IN YOUR SAILS.
EXPLORE. DREAM. DISCOVER
MARK TWAIN
Author & Humorist

43

Lost Without Translation

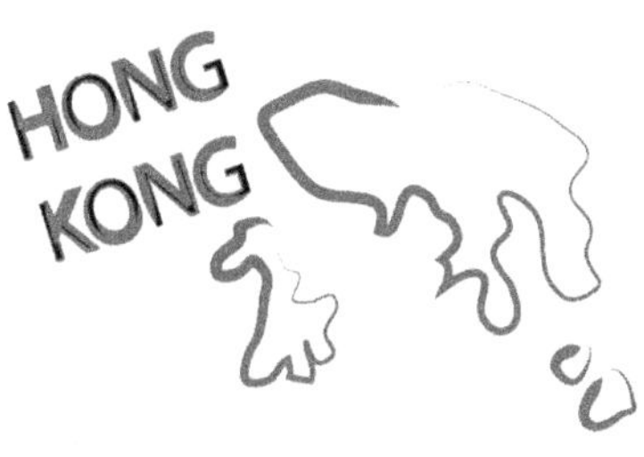

And now for a little family history. My father moved to the United States from Hong Kong in the early 1960s to go to college. Hong Kong, as I'm sure you know, was under British control at that point, and so my dad spoke English fluently. Confident in his ability to speak the same language of the States, my dad had no qualms in studying in America. Upon arriving in San Francisco, he immediately boarded a train to travel to what would be his home for the next several years: Arkansas. As you might imagine, metropolitan Hong Kong and small-town Arkansas are dissimilar in… oh, just about every way.

Shortly after checking in at his university, and in order to achieve a more natural state, my dad set out to investigate his new surroundings. My dad was the adventurous sort, and in spite of the total lack of familiarity, he summoned up his courage and stepped out the door to explore. And so one of my dad's first stops in the United States was a small grocery store, of the Mom-and-Pop variety, where

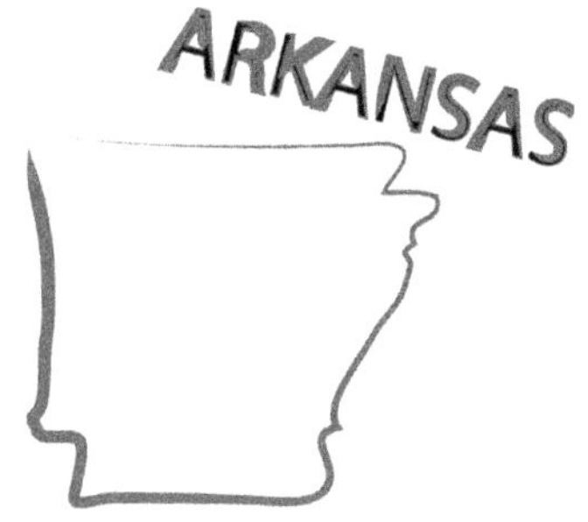

he purchased some food to take back to his dorm room. The aforementioned Pop couldn't have been nicer as my dad paid his bill and turned to walk out the front door.

"Y'all come back now," Pop drawled as a friendly invitation for future business.

My dad hesitated for a moment with his hand on the knob and then turned around and walked back to the counter. The grocer frowned in confusion. "Did you need something else?" he asked my dad. To which my dad, equally confused, replied, "Umm… no. You told me to come back. So I did."

Even though my dad and the grocer both spoke English, they weren't speaking the same language.

The same failure to communicate can happen with us as artists and especially those artists who are immersed in a Christian subculture. It is easy for us, as we speak the same language as the people around us, still to be saying things that they cannot possibly understand.

At the core of artistry is communication, even if what is being expressed is camouflaged. If we fail to communicate with our audience in ways that preserve the possibility of understanding, then we have in many ways failed at our craft. It is far too easy for us to slip into our own Christian lingo, which may work very well in certain limited environments, but which will usually cause the members of any broader audience to simply walk away scratching their heads, leaving them no better off than they were before.

Even worse, it also creates the risk of us falling into one of the cardinal sins for any artist: the sin of cliché.

As artists, this is our challenge. We must discover how to communicate deep, central truths in new and meaningful ways, without defaulting to phrases only we can understand. This is vitally important, because it is possible to speak a shared language while communicating nothing at all.

PRECISION OF COMMUNICATION IS IMPORTANT, MORE IMPORTANT THAN EVER, IN OUR ERA OF HAIR TRIGGER BALANCES, WHEN A FALSE OR MISUNDERSTOOD WORD MAY CREATE AS MUCH DISASTER AS A SUDDEN THOUGHTLESS ACT.

JAMES THURBER

Author, Playwright & Cartoonist

44

What Do You Have In Your Hand?

One of the cruelest parts of having an artistic vision, or even further still, any vision whatsoever, is that we can find ourselves stymied by a lack of resources to make that vision a reality. I'm willing to guess that each of you has something that you would like to achieve as an artist – a screenplay, a film, a score, a performance, or something else – but you hesitate to take that first step forward because you lack what you think you need – money, time, an agent, collaborators, or *whatever* – in order to fully accomplish it.

And so with no step forward, you continually find yourself in the same place.

I suppose there can be some wisdom in first determining what is necessary to achieve a calling. Jesus warned against building a tower without first considering what it would cost to complete it (Luke 14). But keep in mind that Jesus actually was using a metaphor for our spiritual lives, a cautionary word picture to remind us that following our spiritual calling is going to require great sacrifice. But He *wasn't* saying that we should fail to embark on that calling altogether.

I know that at times I have found myself hesitating to step forward creatively or artistically because I lacked the resources

I thought I needed, only to find out in the end that I actually had everything necessary to proceed, to take those first few steps, but just didn't have the eyes to recognize it.

Take, just by way of example, the resource of money. How often have you put your artistic goals on hold because you said to yourself, "I don't have enough money"? Money is, of course, a valuable thing to have in this life, and it is even necessary at times – although probably more rarely than we are willing to admit.

Money is power, but it is the lowest form of power. This may strike you as naïve, perhaps, but think about it for a moment. Money is based only on the value that people give it, but clear-thinking people have accomplished so much without it. In fact, in the grand scheme of things, much more has been accomplished without money than has been accomplished with it, and it is a wonder that we continue to make it the linchpin of our endeavors.

Don't get me wrong: money is something. But it isn't everything. The lack of money or any other resource shouldn't keep you from forging ahead in your artistry.

God called Moses to go to Egypt and turn an entire culture on its head, much like what He is calling artists to do today (Exodus 3-4). Moses, in a very human moment of self-doubt, questioned his own ability and resources, much like many of us artists do: "*What if I don't have what it takes to get the job done?*" But instead of giving Moses political power or money or a conquering army to turn the heads of the ruling authorities, God responded with the simple question, "What do you have in your hand?" It just so happened that Moses had a humble shepherd's staff in his hand, so God used that. And He used it to create a new nation and change an entire culture.

God wants to do the same in the calling He has given you. He wants to use what you already have to do a creative thing now. He has equipped you to be an artist today. Don't allow what you don't have to be more powerful than what you do have. Not having something isn't really a barrier to creativity; it's actually an invitation to more creativity.

So you have a creative calling, and you don't know what to do next? Well, what do you have in your hand?

THE CHIEF VALUE OF MONEY LIES IN THE FACT
THAT ONE LIVES IN A WORLD IN WHICH IT IS OVERESTIMATED.
H.L. MENCKEN
Journalist, Essayist & Satirist

45

My Confession

Okay. *Deep breath.* Here I go. The truth is, I've been putting off writing this article for a long, long time. I've started it before on several occasions, but each time I've set it aside with a handwringing sense of futility. It's not because I don't think it's an important topic, because it is. No, the real reason I've been putting off writing this is because I know I don't know the answer to this particular topic, and so I'm not exactly sure what to say about it.

But why should that stop me? There are plenty of people who don't know what they're talking about, and that doesn't keep them from having all sorts of things to say. There are a lot of terms for such people. We give them all sorts of fancy labels to hide their condition: "pundits," "commentators," and "cable news anchors."

But I digress, which in my case is another weak attempt to avoid addressing my deepest flaw. And that flaw is – *another deep breath*:

Perfectionism.

"Oh, is that it?" you ask, maybe a little surprised. "That's not so bad. We thought you were going to say something a whole lot worse. Hate or greed or lust—something like that, perhaps."

But that's the problem: perfectionism really is as bad as all that. It really is. And I too often don't recognize or admit that fact. And that's why I've struggled to write this article. It's not that I don't have anything to say about it; it's only that I'm afraid it won't come out *just right*. It's almost as if I think I can write about the avoidance of perfectionism only once I have mastered it.

That's not going to happen today. So rather than using this article as a screed, I will use it as my confessional. I'll ramble on here about the devastating effect of perfectionism on me, cobbling my thoughts together until it makes some rough sense, hopefully to both of us.

We live in a culture that demands perfection and typically offers only snide or harsh criticism when we don't achieve it. The problem is that our culture, or at least what I consider the exciting part of it, seems to think perfectionism is a *good* thing, and in some cases *the* thing that results in success. I just did a search online, and found all sorts of well-accomplished and well-lit People of Importance who credit perfectionism alone for their accomplishments. It's in the Church too – come on, admit it, you've seen and heard it – and sometimes perfectionism is even worse there, because we find a way to spiritualize it. Or I should say, I do. This is my confessional, after all, not yours.

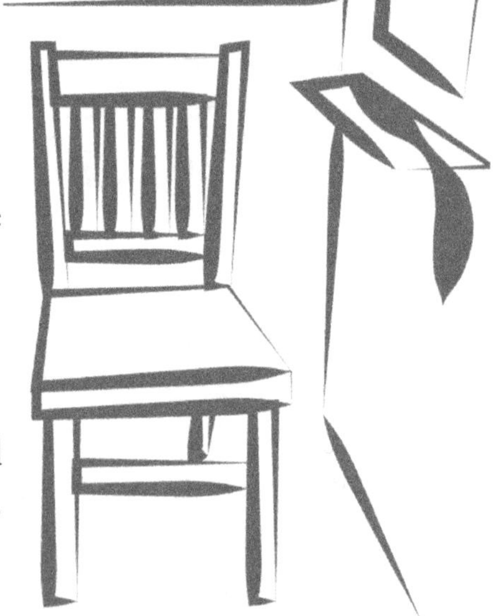

When it comes down to it, I secretly harbor the thought that perfectionism is good, and maybe a lot of artists and creative folks do too. I hold on to the thought that it's my perfectionistic – it's a real word, look it up – habits that motivate me towards success, that all my obsessive compulsions to tweak towards perfection are what make me good at what I do. And in some ways, that's right; those habits and compulsions do indeed drive me to excel. But perhaps it's for the wrong reasons. There is a difference between living and creating by perfectionism and doing the same in the pursuit of excellence. Let's see if I can muddle my way into some sort of understanding here.

It's not that I don't know the difference between perfectionism and the pursuit of excellence—on an intellectual level, I think I do. It's that I don't really know how to parse the two in my own life, how to practice the one without falling prey to the other. It's enough to make me despair, because if there's anything I want, it is to produce art and truth and beauty with that excellence of which my Creator is worthy.

So here is the difference between perfectionism and excellence if I'm just willing to accept it: *Grace.*

Let me put it bluntly: Perfectionism is a denial of grace. It says, "I've got this. I can do it if I just work hard enough." It denies grace for myself and it prohibits grace for others. It is a denial of my absolute fallenness and my absolute need for Him to help me back to my feet. It is a denial of God's role in my artistic process; it is a denial of His role in my life.

That's because perfectionism is a form of self-centeredness

and self-satisfaction. It is a humanistic approach to life and art that draws me further and further into myself, in that it claims in no uncertain terms: *If I will just keep doing everything I can, I will be able to achieve perfection. If I just keep working at this, eventually I will be happy with the outcome, and I will be even happier because I will have made everyone else happy with the outcome as well.* I don't usually say those sentences out loud, but I sure enough think them. You'll notice they are centered entirely around "I" and what "I" is capable of. Perfectionism leaves no room for God's participation, and since God only participates as an act of grace, perfectionism basically is shutting Him out of the process.

Whereas perfectionism is motivated by self-satisfaction, the pursuit of excellence is and should be motivated by worship. The pursuit of excellence is in itself an act of worship. It is an invitation to God to collaborate, an invitation to be involved in the artistic process. It is focused on Him; it is founded in a determination to offer Him the very best I have – and He likes to collaborate in that sort of mess.

As such, abandoning perfectionism in favor of a worshipful pursuit of excellence makes my art *better*, not worse.

The pursuit of perfection wears me out and eventually paralyzes; the pursuit of excellence sets me free into a wide-open field of play. Perfectionism can be my excuse for never getting started, or at least never continuing; the pursuit of excellence gets me going because I can't wait to lay my best at His feet.

Perfectionism is stultifying, and it ruins my relationships, because I start requiring it in and from others—in the misguided belief that I can or have attained it myself. Perfectionism, therefore, is just as much a sin as is fornication or lying or greed. I just overlook it because it's dressed up better.

And when I do see it in myself, I rationalize it: *I'm not* really *being a perfectionist. I'm just trying to be good enough for God.* But then I discover myself in a place where "good enough" is never good enough. By not being honest with myself, I fall deeper into that sin, so far that I lose my ability to tell perfection or excellence apart. And when nothing is "good enough," I lose the satisfaction of the good I have done.

Perfectionism proceeds under the false assumption that I even *know* what perfection is or what it looks like. To paraphrase another writer, perfection is a moving target. As far as we're concerned here on earth, the definition of perfection changes from day to day, all because in our true fallenness, we've lost a clear sight of He Who is Perfect, and resort to guessing.

Perfectionism is rooted in the fear that if I let down my guard, even for a moment, my art will no longer be considered good, that I will subject myself to the death by a thousand cuts that is criticism. That fear ends up binding me up, dictating my every decision and move.

And so I return to it here: there is only one thing that will rescue me from the tyrannical bonds of perfectionism, and that is Grace. Then and only then will I be able to create what is in my heart, rather than what is in the heart of someone else.

Some of you have known nothing but criticism all your life. To you I offer, with any spiritual authority I have been given: *Grace and peace.* Some of you have known nothing but how to give criticism all your life. To you I say as well: *Grace and peace.*

I'm looking back at what I've written here. I don't know if I've done a good job communicating anything. It's too long, too rough, too… something. But maybe I need to allow myself to not be perfect. Maybe I need to make room for the imperfection and worship in it anyway. *Deep breath.* Maybe I need to stop writing and let it be

I'M NOT A PERFECTIONIST AT ALL. I FIND PERFECTIONISTS BORING BECAUSE THE REAL CREATIVE HEART IS IN THE MESS SOMEWHERE.
DAVID MORRISSEY
Actor, Screenwriter & Filmmaker

46
The Turndown

There are many pieces of advice that float around Hollywood, lots of tips and conventional wisdom on how to make it in the arts & entertainment industry. Some of them are good, some of them are wrong, and some of them are just silly. Discernment, I believe, is being able to know which is which. After all, if you're not careful, that nugget of wisdom you have been offered may turn out to be fool's gold.

I've been a professional actor for about eight years, and I've received a lot of good advice in that time. So let me give you one of the best pieces of advice I've ever received, which came early in my creative career. At a crowded industry event, I was sitting next to a fairly successful writer who had befriended me. At some point in the evening, he turned to me and offered this unsolicited word of wisdom: *Never forget the power of saying "no."*

That little gem has served me well on more than one occasion. As artists, it's easy to succumb to the fear that suggests that you'll miss your big break if you say "no" to any opportunity that is set before you. All fears masquerade as Reason – and this one is no exception. It is just quiet enough to keep you from recognizing it for what it is, but just loud enough to mask the voice of your true beliefs. It urges you to be practical, rather than wise. It drives you to say "yes" to anything and everything – even to those opportunities that violate your conscience, that harm you or others on some level, or that God has already told you to decline.

Sometimes we accept opportunities we should turn down because we're afraid of what people will think of us. Sometimes we say "yes" because we are afraid we're turning down the project that will serve as the stepping-stone to the thing we really want to do. Sometimes we say "yes" because we hear the threat, actual or implied: *You'll never work in this town again!* But when you really think about it, none of these are terribly good reasons to say "yes."

The reality is that there is a tremendous amount of power in saying "no." People actually have *more* respect for you professionally and personally when you turn down an opportunity for the right reasons, even if it is an unspoken, begrudging respect. True, after you decline a person's proffered opportunity, he may not ask you again to work with him, but you will be able to live with yourself. Saying "no" for the right reasons is part of what makes you a professional.

More importantly, we should never let that kind of fear determine what our course of action should be. Overcoming that fear requires taking a stand, but stands like that are what make you a stronger artist. If you say "yes" to anything, you are surrendering your artistic integrity to other people to control, and that only makes you weaker, not stronger. You become less, not more.

Some people say "yes" all the time because they believe that graciousness requires it of them. This is a mistake both in practice and in theology. Even Jesus recognized that some situations call for you to say an emphatic "no" and then stick to it. (Matt. 5:37) It is possible for you to say "no" graciously.

But the fear is still there: *What if I miss that golden opportunity to break into the industry?* The truth of the matter is that God is bigger than your ability to miss opportunities, especially when you're trying to honor and obey Him. He does not have a limited supply of opportunities for you. If your calling to be a creative professional is truly from Him, He'll give you what you need to make that calling happen. He is certainly big enough and gracious enough to provide all the opportunities you need to fulfill His purposes for you.

So if you're faced with an opportunity that you believe you shouldn't take, know that you have permission to decline. Saying "no" could be the open door you've been looking for.

DON'T JUST GRAB THE FIRST THING THAT COMES BY.
KNOW WHAT TO TURN DOWN.
WILL ROGERS
Actor, Performer & Humorist

47

My Thanksgiving

I don't feel thankful today. There, I said it. I'm not complaining here, it's just that, as we approach Thanksgiving, that day that kicks off the long, downward glide into Christmas and the end of the year, I take a look around at my circumstances, root around in the ol' emotional cellar, and… nope, I don't feel thankful.

Now, I know that there is a lot to be thankful for in this world of mine, some wonderful things that are happening. In fact, there's probably more than I am capable of seeing. But the fact of the matter is that I've got a lot on my plate, all of which I'd gladly trade for another belt size of turkey, mashed potatoes, and my mother's secret recipe for stuffing. I glance around, and yep, there's a lot to weigh me down. I still need to put together the details of the production program I'll be running next year, handle fundraising for two organizations, come to terms with a close friend after that argument we just had, and figure out how I can get home for Christmas. I'm in an industry plagued by flagging productions, self-aggrandizement, rejection, and vice. Along with the geese, the economy has gone south. People are losing their jobs, their homes, and their loved ones. Friends are watching dreams die. It seems like so much around us is in complete disarray.

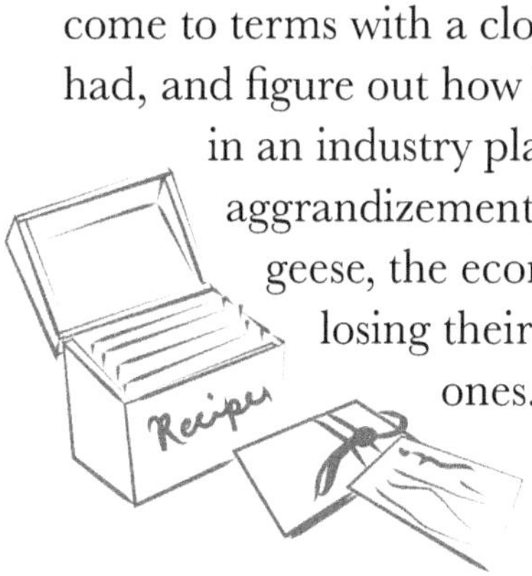

So let's get it out on the table: I don't feel very thankful right now. Maybe you don't feel very thankful either. And yet…

Thank you, Lord.

You see, God didn't call us to *feel* thankful in all circumstances; He called us to give thanks in all circumstances (1 Thess. 5:18). He handed us the easier task of giving thanks, which is a good thing, because I don't think that any of us is capable of feeling thankful all the time. This is a distinction that is especially important for us artists to understand, as we too often tend to let our emotions dictate our reality.

Actually, God created us to have it the other way around. In his book, *Proust Was a Neuroscientist*, author Jonah Lehrer notes, "[T]he mind can induce its own emotions." Our recognition of reality, of that which is true, can determine our emotions. That is to say, giving thanks, whether we feel it or not, is the predecessor to feeling thankful.

If your world seems chaotic and painful right now, I'm in no way minimizing that fact. If I'm to be honest, I've got a bit of that going on myself. But now that we've got that all out in the open, let's turn our faces to the Son, close our eyes, take a deep breath, and…

Thank you, Lord... thank you.

FOR EVERY MOMENT OF JOY, EVERY HOUR OF FEAR
FOR EVERY WINDING ROAD THAT BROUGHT ME HERE
FOR EVERY BREATH, FOR EVERY DAY OF LIVING
THIS IS MY THANKSGIVING.
DON HENLEY
Singer-Songwriter & Musician

48

Snow Days

It's raining in Los Angeles as I start to write this. For those of you who don't live in or near L.A., you should know that this significantly shifts the atmosphere of this place, and for many, it is a welcome change.

I moved to Los Angeles from Omaha, Nebraska, a number of years ago. I am tremendously glad to be here, a city where creativity is valued, but I do miss several things about Omaha: my friends and family, the window-rattling thunderstorms that sweep in from the southwest in the middle of the night, and tickets behind home plate at the College World Series at Rosenblatt Stadium (which is now no longer even standing). But in the time I've been here in L.A., I've found that there is one thing I miss from the Midwest for which there is no substitute: snow days.

When a big snowstorm sweeps across the plains, dumping inches, if not feet, of snow everywhere, it brings the entire metro area to a halt. As a kid, I would get up earlier than I would on any other school day just to find out if school was closed so I could go back to bed again, an action that, in retrospect, defies logic. Even as an adult, I would relish those mornings I'd wake up and observe with a satisfied sigh that deep blanket of white. It was as if, by unspoken and mutual agreement, the entire population understood that it was in each citizen's best interests to fix a pot of coffee, start the fireplace up, and sit down with a good book. And so, along with the snow, a sense of rest would settle over the city.

Rest is not something that happens in Hollywood much. We don't have snow days, and the rain doesn't slow anyone down – in fact, judging by some of the good people on the freeways today, it may just speed them up. The closest thing we have to a snow day is a good-sized earthquake, but I can't see myself praying as earnestly for one of those as I did for snow as a child, not even for the sake of rest. Not that an earthquake ever brought anyone any rest.

But the fact is that we *need* rest. After all, God created the Sabbath rest for us for that very reason. I sheepishly will admit that I, like many of you in the arts and entertainment business, have been guilty of falling into the fear that if I take a little break I may miss my Big Break. I get caught in the mistaken belief that if *I'm* doing nothing, then nothing is happening.

That belief can't be very complimentary to a heavenly Father who reminds us in Psalm 121 that He is taking care of everything for each of us, with no need for sleep or slumber. It's as if He issued the Matthew 11:28 call to all of us who are weary, offered us rest, and we declined.

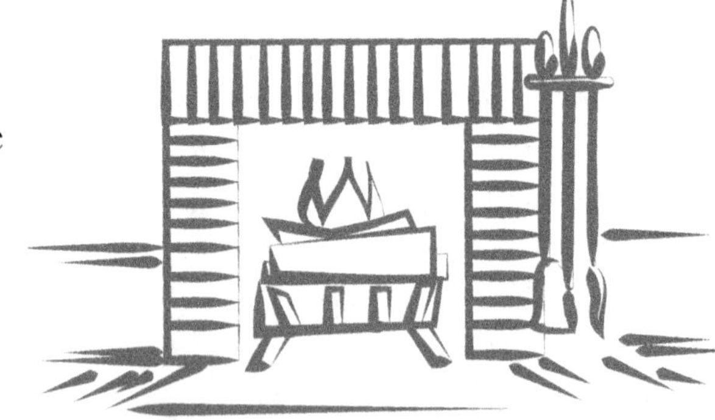

The truth is that we were created to have rest, both as an act of faith and as a matter of necessity. And when we don't get that rest, everything suffers, including our ability to create art and to entertain. In fact, I've had the opportunity to see my productivity and creativity plummet when I'm not taking the time to rest. Conversely, when I get the rest I need, it is like hitting the reset button – physically, emotionally, intellectually, spiritually, and creatively.

Believe it or not, you're built the same way. So if you're ready for the reset, schedule a snow day for yourself. The rest you get will be worth the effort.

TAKE REST;
A FIELD THAT HAS RESTED YIELDS A BOUNTIFUL CROP.
OVID
Poet & Author

49

What? Me Worry?

I've been spending a bit too much time in the dentist chair recently. Don't get me wrong – I've got a kind and competent dentist, and together we're working towards a million-dollar smile that would make any good leading actor's ego swell dramatically. But lately it seems like I've gotten a little too familiar with staring up at the drab, acoustical ceiling tiles, my face stuffed with cotton, and the terror-inducing whine of dental instruments starting up somewhere behind me.

When you begin to recognize which tools are your friends and which ones are about to test your pain threshold, you know you've been sitting there way too long (and may have had one too many shots of novocaine).

A year or so ago, I went to a dentist whom I had not seen before, and as I sat there in his chair, supine, mouth agape, I listened to him calmly relay his assessment of each tooth to his assistant.

"Overall condition of the gums are good," he intoned. *Pause.* "Previous fillings on numbers two, fifteen, eighteen, thirty-one." *Pause.* "The patient frets."

What? I wanted to ask, but couldn't because I had a

periodontal probe and most of the dentist's left hand in my mouth – no, seriously, if I had swallowed hard, he probably would have lost his wristwatch. *The patient* – meaning me, of course – *frets*? Well, yeah, maybe, but how did my *dentist* know? Isn't that more appropriately within the field of study for a psychologist or counselor or someone like that?

It turns out that a dentist can tell when someone is the fretting type (and by that I mean a worrier, not a guitarist) by looking at your teeth. When you fret or worry, you tend to grit and grind your teeth, typically in your sleep, which over time can wear down the enamel on your teeth. And your dentist can tell. This grinding is also known as *bruxism*, which I know mostly because Google told me so.

It turns out that when we worry, it *shows*. It affects everything we do – from the quality of our art to our relationships, from our business decisions to how we sleep at night. If you haven't already experienced this, I'm certain a good Internet search will back me up on that one too.

In Psalm 37:8, we're reminded not to fret because it will only lead to harm, and I'm pretty sure that the Psalmist was speaking of more than just damage to our teeth. With so many anxiety-inducing pressures surrounding us in the arts & entertainment world, however, his admonition may seem at times like an impossible task. Don't fret? Are you kidding me, Mr. Psalmist? I don't think you understand what you're asking for here… I'm in the *entertainment industry*, for goodness's sake, and I have to prepare for that big audition or cover rent or find an even better manager or fire one of my production assistants or fix that relationship with my friend or pay for those ever-growing dentist bills.

Don't fret. It's a simple command in a complex world, a world filled with stress and tension, and you would be right in dismissing the possibility of fulfilling that command if there was no better place to put our worries. But we are assured that there is a better depository for those worries if we are humble enough to put them there:

> *Humble yourselves, therefore, under God's mighty hand, that he may lift you up in due time. Cast all your anxiety on him because he cares for you. (1 Peter 5:6-7)*

How odd that our first and best resort is who we turn to last and only when things are at their worst. It takes humility to admit we're not able to deal completely with the anxieties this world hands us, but in reality, the more we try to carry these burdens on our own, the more harm we do and the more gnashing of teeth we have to endure. We simply were never created to carry these worries in the first place.

So whatever anxieties you are carrying right now – be they in your art, your business, your relationships, or any other area – toss them on God as His responsibility. But whatever you do: *Don't fret. He cares for you.*

WORRY DOES NOT EMPTY TOMORROW OF ITS SORROW;
IT EMPTIES TODAY OF ITS STRENGTH.
CORRIE TEN BOOM
Author & Holocaust Survivor

50

Glitter and Gold

Hollywood is known more for its myth than for its reality, at least in the eyes of the general public. For those who know Hollywood, it draws to mind that truism that "all that glitters is not gold." The substance doesn't always measure up to the presentation. Once the cameras and spotlights and red carpets have been removed, it isn't always the nicest place in the world. In fact, Hollywood can be downright ugly at times.

Walking down Hollywood Boulevard can be a bit anti-climactic and even disillusioning. For the uninitiated, it's as if the curtain has been pulled back and the wizard turns out, in a wearying sort of way, to be much less than anticipated. Although the powers-that-be have tried to clean Hollywood up a bit, this boulevard is populated by people of all sorts: prostitutes and drug addicts, religious peddlers and panhandlers, and even a few actors. The tourist shops are interspersed with the occasional adult bookstore or occult novelty shop. There is garbage, urine, and pollution.

Early in my acting career, I'd see all of this in the evening as I strolled to my scene study class, which met weekly in a studio just off of Hollywood Boulevard. The class itself was made up of quite an assorted bunch as well. One of the students worked as a bartender at the Playboy Mansion.

Another was a dancer for the Los Angeles Lakers. The teacher's language was, well, it was pretty colorful – although I probably should note that the color was usually one shade of blue or another.

Strangely enough, those people turned out to be some of the kindest and most genuine people I've known. There was an *authenticity* to many of them that was oddly compelling. Yes, off-color jokes were told, suggestive clothing was worn, swear words were… sworn. But there was a friendly camaraderie between us, and together, we were each attempting to discover what it means to be an actor as an artist. I liked the process, and still do. I liked those people, and even – oh, wow, please take this the right way – preferred them at times. I began to find gold beneath the glitter.

I suppose that right here would be a good place for me to insert an anecdote about how I stood on my chair, informed my fellow students of their problems, and called them to repentance and holiness. I mean, isn't it my duty to set them straight? But even though my eyes were open for such an opportunity, it did not occur – at least, not in my acting class. I feel okay about that. There is a time for reproach, but apparently, that wasn't it.

I've been slowly learning the art of grace, the art of intentionally inserting into each situation the grace that lives inside of me by the Holy Spirit. An act of kindness to somebody in need, an encouragement to someone else who is feeling down, a short word of wisdom from my limited supply, sometimes just a smile. I think that, like a painter with her brush, we have to learn to apply this grace with discerning strokes and swirls, painstakingly mixing the colors into the details, a touch here, a touch there, until – *presto change-o!* – beauty suddenly emerges where once there was chaos or ugliness.

I'm coming to find, as I move about here among the artists and actors, that being right is not the answer. Not that being theologically and morally correct isn't a goal – it's still important. But I've seen some people who, as they pointed out the wrongness of a particular action or inaction, were the ones who actually had become the monsters. I have to admit that I've been guilty of this as well. Like a horrifying werewolf emerging in the light of a full moon, I have howled my indignation at a person's wrongdoing, repeatedly slashed them to pieces with my call to holiness, and left them dying as I lurched onward, a proud, lycanthropic smile on my face.

It is a little too easy to just be right, although there are many who have missed the mark here as well, myself included. It is much more difficult to be right and to extend grace. Not the sloppy "live and let live" kind of grace of turning a blind eye to sin, but grace that is extended in a very real, proactive sense. Without doing so, the best we can hope for is to be horribly right.

That is because holiness without grace is not holiness. To be right without the extension of grace is to be wrong.

TO DESIRE AND EXPECT NOTHING FOR ONESELF AND TO HAVE PROFOUND SYMPATHY FOR OTHERS IS GENUINE HOLINESS.
IVAN TURGENEV
Novelist & Playwright

51

The Power of a Quiet Song

It was Christmas Eve, 1818, in a small alpine village in Austria, where a poor priest named Joseph Mohr approached Franz Gruber, his friend and the town headmaster, with a pressing request. Mohr had recently discovered that the organ at his St. Nicholas Church was broken, and without it, there would be no music for his congregation's Christmas Eve service that night. So with a sense of urgency, Mohr handed Herr Gruber a three-stanza poem he had written, with the request to compose a song to be played on the guitar. Gruber sat down and quickly composed *Stille Nacht*, or in English, *Silent Night.*

And from such desperate and humble beginnings, much like those of the King to whom Mohr's lyrics referred, came the song that was to become one of the most beloved of all Christmas carols.

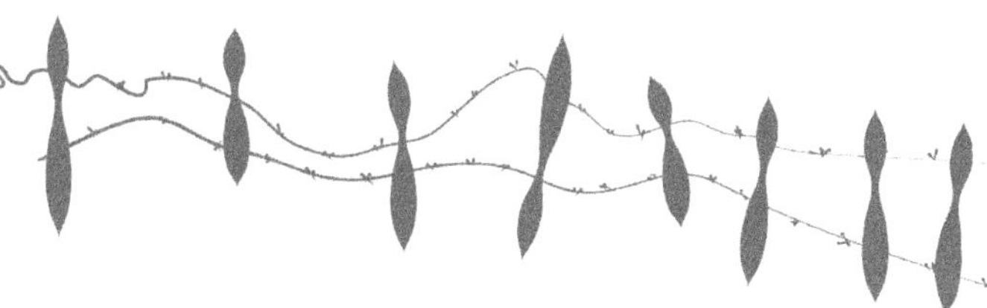

It was Christmas Eve, 1914, and the Great War that would one day be known as World War I had been raging for over six months. The weary soldiers on both the German and British sides of the Western Front – fathers and uncles, brothers and sons – huddled in the cold, wet darkness of their muddy trenches. Their superior officers had ordered, very specifically and very sternly, that there would be no truce for Christmas – the battle was to wage on. Somewhere in the stillness of the night, however, a soldier began to sing an old, familiar carol, *Silent Night*, the melody wafting through the air to his enemies' ears. A second voice joined in, and then another. Against their superior officers' orders, soldiers up and down the front lines began to sing the song together – some in German, some in English. Imagine that: enemies singing together in the middle of a war. Bravely, the men from both sides crept out of their shadowy trenches and into the war-ravaged area in the middle known as No Man's Land, where they gathered and celebrated Christmas together, giving small gifts of coffee, cigarettes, and candy to one another, mourning each other's losses, and singing of the God whose heavenly peace could bring an end to all war.

It was, in the words of Sir Arthur Conan Doyle, who later wrote of the event, "one human episode amid all the atrocities which have stained the memory of the war."

It was Christmas Eve, 2002, and a small group of songwriters and musicians trudged through the snow to gather in a rustic bar in Omaha, Nebraska, to perform a few songs they had written. The audience members, by all appearances, were as rough as the bar in which they sat, and one could see their lives etched in the hard lines of their faces as they listened to the tunes and politely applauded after each one. At the end of the evening, the last performer standing on the stage finished his final song and looked out over the crowd. Without much forethought, he began to play on his guitar the chords of a familiar hymn, almost two hundred years old. A holy hush crept over that ragtag audience as, one by one, these strangers joined together to sing *Silent Night.*

From there on the stage, I watched the soft, and perhaps wistful, light enter those eyes as God once again drew near to mankind.

And so we see that such is the power of God through a song – or through a painting, a film, a photograph, a poem, or any other piece of art that communicates the nature of beauty and the beauty of nature, all of which flows from and reflects the Giver of all good things. In this world that is subjected to the unraveling effect of time, it is what makes art good and what makes good art essential.

We live in a society whose fascination with power has seeped into the very fabric of its culture, like water creeping up a piece of cloth when its edge is dipped in a pool. We see this fascination in business and politics, we see it in the arts and entertainment, we even see it in the modern Church. We somehow have come to equate power with position, volume, visibility, and wealth, and so we too often grasp for more of those as we misidentify them as the power of God.

And yet, so little of that was present that powerful First Night.

History, we rediscover time and again, offers insight to our future without determining what it will be. This world of ours, in all its fallen weariness, will continue to provide us – no, it will continue to thrust upon us – what can only be described as brokenness, whether it is a broken organ, or a broken war, or broken lives. And yet, over and over, history still reveals to us the God who bows low to touch us, to bind us together. History reveals to us the God who offers the simple, yet overarching, promise of future silent nights through the life of a bawling baby who arrived, with no worldly fanfare, in a sleepy town in the Middle East. History reveals the God who gently shakes us awake to whisper His Word made flesh:

Emmanuel. God is with us.

EXCEPT THE CHRIST BE BORN AGAIN TONIGHT
IN DREAMS OF ALL MEN, SAINTS AND SONS OF SHAME,
THE WORLD WILL NEVER SEE HIS KINGDOM BRIGHT.
VACHEL LINDSAY
Poet

52

The End of the Story

I have a good friend who has what I, as a self-proclaimed film aficionado, consider to be a near fatal flaw. (I won't tell you his name, mostly because he'll be reading this. You know who you are…) This friend of mine hates to talk about movie details or plot lines to *any* degree before he has seen the movie himself. He just doesn't want to know. Some flimflam about spoiling the experience for him by finding out how any of the story goes. I know you're thinking the same thing I am – he's crazy, right?

As an actor and producer, I read a lot of screenplays, both new ones and those that have already been made. Not only are they a good form of cheap entertainment, not only do they inspire and fire the imagination, but they can teach something on a deeper level as well.

One that I finished a while ago is the screenplay for the movie *Big Fish*. The story, in a nutshell – and I don't think I'm spoiling anything for those of you who haven't seen it because this premise is set out near the beginning of the film (unless you're the aforementioned Crazy Friend of mine, in which case, please stop reading now and go rent the movie) – is the life in retrospective of a man named Edward, who, as a young boy, had the opportunity to see how he was going to die later in life. Rather than get upset about this revelation, he decides that he can live his life absolutely free from fear. In his words:

```
                EDWARD
I mean, on one hand, if death was all
you thought about, it could kind of
screw you up. But it could kind of
help you, couldn't it? Because you'd
know that everything else you can
survive.
```

Edward goes on to experience incredible adventures in life because he knew how he was going to die. He knew how his story would end, and that gave him the courage and the faith to live the middle of his story, complete and without fear, compromise, or regret.

This is one of those plots that I wish I had thought of first, not only for a screenplay, but also for my own life.

It reminds me a bit of the similar biblical storyline of the Apostle Peter in Acts 12, in which we find our hero in jail, chained between two guards, and for all practical purposes, facing death the next morning (after all, the villain, Herod, had killed Peter's buddy, James, just a short time earlier, and probably had arrested Peter for the same reason). So we join our hero on the last night of his life, under lock and key, and he is… sound asleep. So sound asleep, in fact, that the angel who comes to rescue him has to knock him around a little to wake him up.

I don't know about you, but if it was the night before I was going to be killed, I'd be spending some serious time in prayer, trying to persuade God to get me out of the jam into which somehow He had let me wander. I certainly wouldn't be able to sleep.

Maybe Peter was just crazy. Or narcoleptic. After all, he did seem to fall asleep at the most inopportune times, didn't he? On the Mount of Transfiguration. In the Garden of Gethsemane. Perhaps, however, our hero's ability to sleep so peacefully this time was really because he already knew how his story ended, and he realized that this wasn't it.

We have to go back in time to find this out, however. In John 21:18, Jesus says to Peter something to the effect of: "When you were young, you could go anywhere you wanted, but *when you get old*, you're going to be taken places you don't want to go." In effect, Jesus was telling Peter that he was going to get old, and that he wouldn't die until after he did.

Meanwhile, back at the prison cell – Peter could snooze away, knowing that he would not die until sometime down the road when he got old. Huh. How about that? Not only can you stand on the promises of God, you can sleep on them too. How's that for knowing how the story goes?

I wonder what my life would be like if I lived as if I truly believed what God has told me about how my story will go. I wonder what Grand Decisions I might make, what Incredible Adventures I might go on if I took the time to find out what promises God has for me and then lived as if I believed Him. How would this world be different?

I have a feeling I will live more daringly when I completely believe that God will supply all my needs according to His riches in glory in Christ Jesus. I will leap more eagerly when I entirely grasp that He looks to strongly support those whose hearts are completely His. I will stride more confidently when I understand that this is indeed my Father's world and I walk with His authority as His son. When I understand that this, after all, is how the story goes…

> *The people who know their God shall be strong, and carry out great exploits. (Daniel 11:32)*

Knowing how this story goes just might enable us to live out our lives complete and without fear, compromise, or regret.

And perhaps get us a good night's rest in the process.

WHAT A FOOL, QUOTH HE, AM I, THUS TO LIE IN A STINKING DUNGEON, WHEN I MAY AS WELL WALK AT LIBERTY! I HAVE A KEY IN MY BOSOM, CALLED PROMISE, THAT WILL, I AM PERSUADED, OPEN ANY LOCK IN DOUBTING CASTLE.

JOHN BUNYAN
Preacher & Novelist

Shun Lee Fong is a writer, actor, filmmaker, musician, and former attorney. He is the founder and creative director of The Greenhouse Arts & Media, a creative arts organization located in Los Angeles, California, where he runs Genuine Productions, LLC, a media production company that focuses on film, publishing, new media, and other creative platforms. He also teaches entertainment law & ethics at a number of universities and makes himself available as a creative consultant for both individuals and organizations.

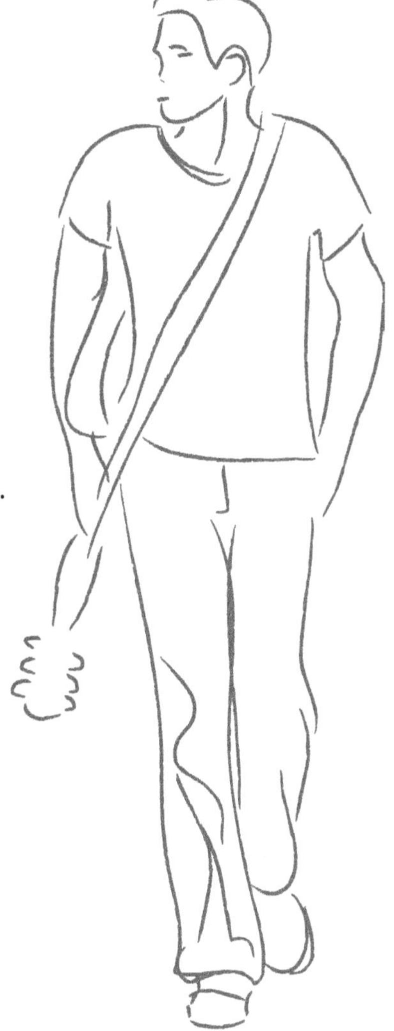

For workshops and public speaking engagements, contact Shun Lee at shunlee@greenhouseproductions.com.

Find him online at:

Website: www.shunlee.com
Facebook: @shunlee
Twitter: @Shun_Lee
Instagram: @shunleefong

Also available for purchase:
The Saints & The Poets
Travel Companion

THE PEOPLE WHO KNOW THEIR GOD SHALL BE
STRONG, AND CARRY OUT
GREAT EXPLOITS.
DANIEL 11:32B

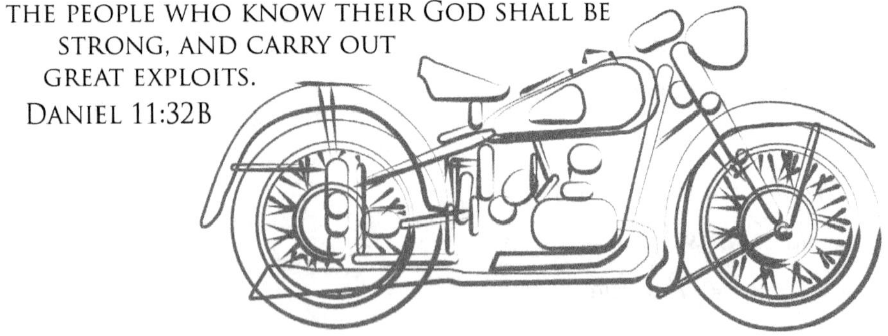

www.ingramcontent.com/pod-product-compliance
Lightning Source LLC
LaVergne TN
LVHW020715110826
845149LV00012B/2277

* 9 7 8 0 9 9 6 3 6 7 5 2 3 *